WHA'
BELIEVE

Spiritual Contemplations
For One's Soul

JOSANNE RENE ROJAS

ISBN: 978-0-578-29961-7 (Paperback)

Front cover image by Kamaljeet Singh
Book design by Kamaljeet Singh

Printed the United States of America.

Disclaimer: The publisher and the authors do not make any guarantee or other promise as to any results that may be obtained from using the content of this book. This publication is meant as a source of valuable information for the reader, however it is not meant as a substitute for direct expert assistance. If such level of assistance is required, the services of a competent professional should be sought.

Dedication

First and foremost, this book is dedicated to God. My assignment would not have been possible, without the prodding and wisdom of the Holy Spirit, and for that I feel immensely blessed. This assignment has definitely taught me about radical obedience and the mercies engrained in God's expeditious grace.

Secondly, this is a literary compendium on belief for the spirit man so my book is dedicated to all those who dare to read from the spirit and jump over the carnal limitations of their mind. For all those holding my book in their hands, in-print or electronically, I urge you to read with intention and expectation because this book was destined to be read by you. God has ordained this time and season for you to take a conscientious look at your beliefs. It is not by chance that I was given this assignment, and it is not by chance that you have been positioned to read this book to assist you in completing yours. Remember dear reader, your decisions decide your destiny, so make a decision today to read and believe God.

With lots of ♥ from me to you!

P.S. To my very close friends and family, you will have to read the book first to know just how much of a dedication this is to you as well!!! ♥ ♥ ♥

CONTENTS

SPIRITUAL CONTEMPLATIONS FOR ONE'S SOUL!

FOREWORD

It was few seconds to midnight on the 31st of December 2009, when I felt a touch that woke me from the bed, the sick bed. While other people were in church - presenting their New Year's resolutions before God, I was alone at home lying on a sick bed.

Though I didn't know who or what touched me, I heard a voice that told me to check the time. And behold, when I did, it was midnight.

The voice asked, "What is your New Year's resolution?". "I want to be closer to God in the New Year," was my response. After all, what else could a young boy who had been sick all year ask for? Like Josanne, I knew church, but I couldn't say the same for God. I wasn't sure what that resolution meant, but I hoped it would at least deliver me from the destruction that was stirring me.

To be honest, if anybody had told me back in 2009 that I would become anything at all, I would have rebuked the person. Maybe the person would have even become my worst enemy.

Prior to that time, I hawked sachet water across the streets of Lagos, Nigeria. It was a full-time job during the holidays, but when school was in session, I'd get to it immediately after school hours, daily. I would hide whenever I sighted a familiar face, especially my classmates, because those who saw me hawking did not hesitate to mock me in class the next day. Hawking sachet water was my way of supporting my parents who, at the time, were not doing well.

So that's right, I didn't believe this world had a place for me. I believed I had to struggle in a world that was already a struggle. I believed that the sickness was a sign that I was about to leave this world. I believed that my self-righteousness would earn me a place at the top; little did I know, that this world had no place for self-righteous people.

That was my problem right there, my beliefs! I wish a book like this was available back then, my transition would have been smoother. But now that Josanne has yielded to the leading of God to write this, then no one should remain in life's struggle after reading this.

One of the first things that struck me as I read this book was where she revealed the effect of God's curse upon the earth after man fell. If God cursed the earth, can the same earth produce for a man who is not in alignment with God? No way!

My life is a testimony of the depths Josanne unveiled in this book. God has given me a name and a fame in every land where I've been put to shame, just because I forsook those unprofitable beliefs and dared to believe Him.

If you're confused about life and searching for something to help you realign, then you got the right book. If you've been searching for a way to end your struggles, then you just hit a jackpot. And if you've struggled and still struggle with identity, then I couldn't be happier for you; your life is about to experience a turnaround that will surprise you.

Have a good read!

Emeka Anslem
Author/Gospel Media Influencer

PREFACE

$\mathcal{I}$ was mandated to write this book as the year sprouted into 2021. Honestly, God told me since the beginning of that year that my first book would be called "What do you believe?" I did not believe that I was capable of writing a book on belief, especially as I was only beginning to truly challenge the false beliefs that were entrenched in my mind. I told God I never envisioned such a title for my first book and I'd always spoken about writing on my raunchy and exciting past of bad decisions and fruitless ambitions.

Ok! Ok! God was not impressed with the mindset I'd been carrying all along. I truly believe that the eyes of the Lord rolled as I expressed my unrewarding thoughts to Him. Nonetheless, I'd never, for one second, ever envisioned myself writing a book about anything to do with God.

Like many of you, I became engulfed in being too busy to do God's work. Writing became a challenge as I was faced with increasing responsibilities as a mother to a 2 year old and a 10 year old while co-managing a business with my husband. I could not find the time to dedicate to writing my first book and I battled with feeling unqualified and doubtful.

Firstly, who am I to tell people to examine their beliefs; and secondly, why would anyone listen to what I had to say. As someone who shies away from being in the spotlight or in anything that begets attention, I was totally confused about how I could live out my dream of being a writer without being in the spotlight as one.

Every time I faced a challenge throughout the year, God would ask me "What do you believe?" as if I was part and parcel of an invisible jury watching myself stand trial. Eventually, I was dared to examine why I did not believe God's promises for me and this book. The all-knowing God will give us a promise and we would question and doubt Him more than we do anyone else. Aren't we a funny bunch of carnal minded creatures?

While I did not feel qualified to write my God-given assignment, I did feel a burning conviction in the crevices of my heart which sought to remind me that I was duty bound to God's instruction. I decided to start a blog (Spiritual Literacy 101) with the hope that I could accomplish three things:

- Begin overcoming my fear and pure dislike of being seen or known.

- Begin writing because that's what writers do. They write!

- Deepen my understanding of God's Word; and share the revelations and insights found, until I was worded up enough to write on my assignment.

I also hoped that I would at least gain some discipline and consistency in writing and end my terrible relationship with procrastination as well.

After about six months of blogging (still very inconsistent), the month of December had arrived and I was four weeks away from 2022. I still did not know what to write and I really did not have the time to produce a book draft, or so I thought. I'd failed miserably in completing two online writing courses I'd enrolled myself in all year; and I had no idea about the do's and don'ts of writing a book, even though I possessed the talent to write.

I felt empty and unaccomplished and I questioned if God really did tell me that my book would be written in 2021. Maybe it wasn't God, maybe it was my sub-conscience that spoke to me. Nonetheless, I sought to make an appeal to God. I figured that even if God had said that it would be written, faith without works is dead. At the end of the day, I was responsible for putting in the work to manifest what God promised. As you are aware, God is not a genie.

Realizing that I had only myself to blame, I sought to make a new deal with the Lord. I pleaded my case before Him; even giving Him evidence of how busy I'd been with legitimate tasks and how well-intentioned I'd been all year. It seemed like the forces of life had been against me. I told Him that by all reasonable standards, it would be best if we postponed this promise/assignment until 2022, and I would truly commit to getting my book draft done as a matter of priority in the New Year.

For that, I received absolutely no response from the Lord but I comforted myself with the belief that my plea was so reasonable, I would be given the grace to reassign a new timeline to my task because my God is an understanding God.

In the wee hours of the following morning, my throat began to feel funny and it felt like I'd developed an instant dry cough. It was sudden and strange, but I passed it off as having a dry throat and so, I had a drink of water. I'm lying next to my husband and toddler and I am literally holding in my sudden onset of coughs because Covid-19 had been brewing in the atmosphere of my homeland and I did not want to worry my husband.

I got up the next morning and tried to convince myself that it was probably just the flu because besides Covid-19, there was an alleged cold/flu going around. I go to the pharmacy that morning to get some medication and I feel compelled to buy a Covid-19 rapid test. *By now you are guessing the outcome of this bizarre story.* I take the test that afternoon and I am Covid-19 positive. I proceed to take a PCR test to confirm and the next day that comes back positive as well. I was confused about my predicament, and of course, my brain was flustered by a swoon of negative and fearful thoughts since Covid-19 had taken down so many people to their grave.

The Lord finally decided to chime in and speak to me. *Oh yes, now I could hear Him as clear as day!* He reminded me that His promises are sure, and that now I had all the time I needed to complete His book and He expected absolutely no excuses. This was not the grace I'd been expecting, but right then and there I learned a few things about the mercies of God's grace. I truly did not deserve the chance I'd been given but I was so thankful that God humbled me.

Despite me having a terrible cough, I felt absolutely no fear about having the Covid-19 virus thereafter. I knew deep down that I would be fine. If I claim to know God, and believe His words to be true, why would I have any need to fear? Why would God give me grace to complete my overdue assignment and not protect me? After eleven months of uncertainty, I was forced to put pen to paper until all that God deposited within me could be drawn out.

I was placed on quarantine for 21 days and I was self-isolated in my son's room in our home. No one else was positive for the virus. *Imagine that!* I took an arsenal of medication to fight my cough and I committed myself to starting and completing my book. I was intentional and a bit proud that Jehovah Jireh, my provider, remembered me. I felt like the one sheep Jesus left the ninety-nine sheep to look for. God did not write me off as incompetent or incapable. He rescued me from my self-sabotaging ways and I was able to complete my draft manuscript during my period of quarantine. God delivered on His promise of my book being written in 2021. My quarantine ended on Christmas Eve and so did my book's first draft. Right on the cusp of a new year, God showed up to remind me that He is not a man that He should lie. If He says it, He will do it!

This is a simple yet powerful example of God's integrity, and my hope is that this book would empower you to trust in the integrity of God and His Word. With great optimism, I dare you to examine your beliefs and mindsets and see if they are in alignment with what God has said and promised you.

I want you to know that God can rescue you from yourself, and from any unfavorable circumstance, if only you would believe Him and have confidence in His trustworthiness.

This book is for all those who struggle with fulfilling their God-ordained assignments. This book is for the non-believer who feels compelled to question the legitimacy of God and Christianity. This book is for the believer who desires growth in their relationship with Jesus. This book is for anyone who feels a God-ordained purpose flowing through their veins, but battle with the doubts and fears that flood their minds. This book is for anyone in search for answers to their questions. This book is for all those who wish to have their minds transformed.

This book is for YOU!

INTRODUCTION

$\mathcal{J}$ am no expert on the biology and psychosis of belief; however, I do possess a qualification that surpasses any scientist, psychiatrist, or philosopher and that is revelation from the Most High God. You see, God is the mastermind behind all that has been created in the natural and supernatural realms. His thoughts (and ways) remain higher than that of angels, demons, creatures, and men. When He reveals truth, He exposes lies, and oftentimes the subtlety of the many deceptions that masquerade themselves easily as truth.

Kingdom knowledge is key to commanding your God-ordained destiny. By now, you would have read about my sojourn to quarantine for the sole purpose of accomplishing my God-given assignment within God's prescribed timeline. To a carnal-minded man, my story will make absolutely no sense;it may even seem superficial. However, for those who have the spiritual eyes to see and ears to hear, they will understand the revelation of what has been shared.

This book should be read by all those who desire God's revelation. This book will bring illumination to the darkness of sin and unbelief that pervades our minds. Understand that this book is not a full scale solution to all of life's challenges; rather it aims to lead you to the only solution which is Jesus Christ. The inherent mission of this book is to challenge you to self-examine your thoughts and belief systems against the standards of the Kingdom of God and ascertain if you do truly believe in God and what His word says.

I've come to learn that we are all guilty of taking up convictions on the areas of the Bible that are convenient to us and easily doable for us. As for the areas where we may have a weakness or even disagree with God, we tend to skim past them or find contradictory interpretations for them to appease us. We go even further to self impose grace on ourselves for our wrongdoings. We forget that as a Christian, it is not about believing what we think; rather it is about believing what God has said. If God said it, it is so!

When man fell in the Garden of Eden, it was because Eve chose not to believe what God had said; and for that moment, she doubted the integrity of His instruction. Her actions indicated she did not believe God when He said that they would die if they ate or touched the fruit of that tree. Instead, she chose to believe in the devil's deception that the fruit was good for food and wisdom. Further, she doubted God and believed the devil when He said that she would not die.

When we disobey God, we are telling God that we do not agree with His Word and we do not believe in the cause and effect of what He has said. Why then, do we blame God for not stopping the atrocities of men upon men in this world? Why don't we blame ourselves for not believing in all that He has said? Everything we need to know from everlasting to everlasting is written in God's Word. So what's the problem really? The only problem is we simply don't want to believe. Our carnal nature is always ready to ask if God really did say what He said.

I urge you to take your time when reading this book. Don't rush God's revelation; instead make your requests, for understanding, known. God has integrity, so trust Him! Keep a journal and write down every lie in your life that has been exposed and every truth that has been revealed to you. Affirm yourself daily in the promises, prophecies, and principles laid out by God.

Invest time in reading God's Word alongside this reading and I promise you will be filled with light. John 1:5 reads "The light shines in the darkness, and the darkness has not overcome it." If you believe this, you will be comforted by the knowledge that with God's light, your purpose can never be extinguished from this earth.

I pray that God would take any blinders of unbelief off your eyes as you read and that you would walk into the fulfilment of your God-ordained purpose.

Believe God and be blessed!

THERE IS NO GREATER TIME IN THE HISTORY
OF THE UNIVERSE TO BELIEVE IN GOD THAN NOW!

THIS EXACT MOMENT!

I WANT YOU TO KNOW THAT NO MATTER YOUR
AGE, GEOGRAPHIC LOCATION OR CIRCUMSTANCE;
THE GOD WHO IS THE "I AM" HAS MADE
HIS PROMISES AVAILABLE TO YOU RIGHT
AT THIS VERY MOMENT IF ONLY YOU
WOULD CHOOSE TO BELIEVE.

CHAPTER

1

A LITTLE BIT
ABOUT MY JOURNEY

$\mathcal{M}$y inspiration for writing this book was God-given. I take no credit for it; as all the glory belongs to Yahweh. I am simply a mouthpiece and a scribe for all that the Holy Spirit has laid upon my heart and mind. When God called me back into the kingdom family, I had to revisit many of the things I once believed. As I read the Scriptures and grew in my relationship with God, I recognized that my prior life was a wreck because of an extremely skewed belief system about God, Christianity, myself, and life as a whole. The worse thing is to not know that you don't know; and pride and self-righteousness will have you believing that you possess the authority and knowledge to verify your own limited and skewed thoughts as truth.

The Bible emphasizes that Jesus Christ is the way, the truth and the life and so the only verifier we will ever need is Jesus. He not only verifies truth, but He can also show us the way to having eternal life.

For as long as I can remember, I had been perturbed by the fact that I did not know what my earthly purpose entailed. As a child, my existence felt out of place in this world, and I daydreamed more often than not. I was a frequent participant in my own inner conscious world and would zone out time and again amongst companions, strangers, and friends.

I would ask God repeatedly, what the purpose of my creation was, and why He thought it best to place me here. I would sometimes pinch myself and touch objects around me in bewilderment at my being and the reality of this earthly realm. What really confused me as a kid was why I would be punished for my sins when I did not even have a choice in being here. We were pre-destined without any pre-consultation and that did not sit down well with my younger self at all. I felt clueless. Nevertheless, I submerged myself in living for what I thought constituted God's ultimate purpose; however, I really hoped that the Heaven-and-Hell narrative was merely a dream.

When I decided to rededicate my life to Christ in 2018, I knew it was a matter of me going all-in or staying out. Although I spent most of my childhood and teenage years learning and walking in the ways of the church, I did not really have the experience of growing in God.

God began calling me back into His sheepfold in 2017, and I really could not understand why He would be calling and pursuing a wretch like me. Believe me, my past had run its course through several murky waters of sin; so I really did not think that I was qualified or fit to be a Christian. I promised myself to never be a church-going hypocrite.

I always believed that I would one day write an eye bulging drama ridden novel showcasing my numerous escapades growing up with a few life lessons strung in. Imagine my surprise when God told me that my first assignment for the Kingdom was to write a book called "What do you believe?" and to erase every thought I had about using my gift of words to glorify my former life of sin.

Our lives are reflections of our belief systems, and the primary assignment of the Holy Spirit is to recalibrate our belief systems to the mechanics of God's Word, His Spirit, and Truth.

Our minds are the data centres that transmit beliefs. As we transition from childhood into adulthood, we carry forward beliefs that are sometimes false, manipulated, limited, or negative – and these faulty beliefs truncate the promise of God assigned to our lives. It's high risk to believe all of our thoughts without examining

Our lives are reflections of our belief systems, and the primary assignment of the Holy Spirit is to recalibrate our belief systems to the mechanics of God's Word, His Spirit, and Truth.

them according to God's Word. The receptacles in our minds are wired to manifest whatever we believe whether we are conscious of it or not. If we believe in a narrative of failure, failure will follow us; because the receptacles in our minds are wired to manifest our beliefs. God's Word is an apparatus and we can use it daily as our spiritual vacuum to remove the dust particles of sin that contaminate us directly and indirectly.

I was ignorant of how terrible my belief system was until God showed me the connection between my unfulfilled life and my unfulfilling thoughts. The way I thought and the things I believed, especially about God, had always been to my demise. I regret not re-dedicating my life to Christ sooner, as there is so much to learn and do in the Body of Christ in such a short span of time. An extensive amount of time is needed to recondition our minds and bring our thoughts, deeds, and words into alignment with Christ.

I remember getting baptized in my teens and then falling off the train of Christianity after, as I traversed a long path of rebellion. I yearned to be identified as a rebel and if anyone told me to turn right, I would purposefully turn left. I craved to "burn and learn", thinking there was fun to be had in the fire. Unbeknownst to me, I was drowning in the mire and strongholds of so many sins; sexual immorality, drugs, breaking the law, pornography, fighting, unhealthy relationships, self-harm, sexual identity issues and the list goes on. Had it not been for God's gracious hand in my life, I truly believe I was on a path headed for jail or even an untimely death.

Despite my misguided adventure-junkie nature, I was naturally bright and driven. I was able to seamlessly acquire my education and even land a tertiary scholarship. I was a bright girl who thought she knew it all, but was so naïve to the many deceptions that left my life unhinged. I passively went through University, unsure of what I really wanted and why I wanted it. *Actually, I hated University!* My degree in Sociology was boring and uninspiring. I was simply passing time and found more joy on the campus tennis courts than in the classroom.

Soon enough my identity became plagued by my moving from one unhealthy relationship into another, which ultimately meant that I'd migrated from one stronghold to another in the spirit. When two persons who have no identity in Christ come together, they bring together an interconnection of generational curses, iniquities, burdens, strongholds and warped mindsets.

If we do not have our identities rooted in the foundation of Jesus Christ and His Word, we will align ourselves with all that opposes God's perfect will for our lives. *2 Corinthians 6:14 says "Do not be bound together with unbelievers; for what partnership have righteousness and lawlessness, or what fellowship has light with darkness."* Unless we have the light of God shining through us, we will be infected by the darkness that surrounds us.

How can we expect to commit ourselves to persons who do not have the light of God in them and not be infected by the darkness of their values, beliefs, mindsets and proclivities? *John 1:5 says "the light shines in the darkness and the darkness did not comprehend it"* so it was no surprise that when God called me into His light and kingdom, He commanded that I walk away from the toxic relationship I'd been suffering in silence in.

> *How can we expect to commit ourselves to persons who do not have the light of God in them and not be infected by the darkness of their values, beliefs, mindsets and proclivities?*

In my youth I wanted to be identified as a rebel, not understanding that the identity of a rebel represented someone selfish, disobedient, unlawful and unholy. As a young adult, I searched for what I identified as love in the bosom of men and women's darkness. I'd written a myriad of poems about love and how it became a raging ambush on my heart. I spent all those years searching to satisfy my soul in the arms of another, unaware that God's agape love had been right there available to me from the time my life had sprouted from its seed.

> *I spent all those years searching to satisfy my soul in the arms of another, unaware that God's agape love had been right there available to me from the time my life had sprouted from its seed.*

When God called me initially, I did what I'd done all my life: I rebelled. I did not want to be identified as a Christian. At that time, I believed that Christians were hypocrites - pretentious and boring- and I truly cherished my flawed definition of freedom. I did not want to feel conviction when I played Carnival, fornicated, or made my wrong choices. I wanted to continue being seen as "crazy Jo" and as a fun-filled rebel who seemingly had it all figured out. Unbeknownst to everyone, however, I was burning up inside for years with a depressing and sick feeling in my chest, knowing that I was not where I was supposed to be. To some extent, I'd already given up on trying to figure my life out and I'd decided to make the best out of my bad situations and toxic relations.

Listen Up!

When God is in pursuit of you, He will change the hearts of men, shift around your circumstances, and trap you into making an urgent decision to come as you are or turn away from Him. After months of protesting God and asking for more time, I remember God telling me that His hand of protection would be removed from my life if I chose to continue my path of rebellion against His Word. He made it clear that He had a plan for my life and my time to turn off onto the narrow path had come. It was now or never!

My chest was heavy, and my heart was pounding. Do you know how scary it is to live a life without God's grace and mercy? This was no joking matter! My life of foolish adventure and brokenness was now at a dead end. Little did I know, God had brought me to a dead-end to get my attention and I was forced to stop, let go of the steering wheel of my mind and inquire into the Lord's Word.

Rebellion against God's truth and commands is the reason why we are oppressed by our nature of sin. In the Garden of Eden, Eve was deceived and she succumbed to unbelief. She chose not to believe God's commands even if it was just for a moment. That moment catapulted mankind into a death sentence. Where there is sin, there is judgment - even if that sin was well-intentioned.

> *Where there is sin, there is judgment - even if that sin was well-intentioned.*

If it had not been for Jesus Christ's redemptive plan of salvation, where would we be today?

When I surrendered my life to God, He immediately began shifting the people and circumstances in my life around for His greater good. He was on an urgent mission for me to be fast-tracked onto a life of holiness. I was in urgent need of God's blood-washed transformation. My mind was filthy, unprofitable, unclean, unaligned to the Word of God, and limited by a flurry of false beliefs.

As He was leaving no stone unturned in my life, I could sense that God was quickly changing the desires and inclinations of my heart. I began investing in listening to sermons of the greats like T.D. Jakes, Apostle Joshua Selman, Prophetess Juanita Bynum, and Myles Munroe. I began attending conferences and buying spiritually-sound books from great fathers of the faith like A.W. Tozer, C.S. Lewis, and E.W. Kenyon; and I invested time into reading them alongside the Word to give me a greater understanding of who God is.

I'd always been a reading fanatic. My life of lust had been triggered as a young kid by a book called "Canal Fever". It really was a feverish book and I soon advanced to reading the erotic books of Zane. Sin always starts small and then erupts into a mega-fest in your heart. As I got older, I remember becoming engrossed even in the universalistic writings of persons like Paulo Coelho. I revered the writings of Coelho so much, but I'd never taken the time to actually read my Bible in context or at all, so how could I have revered God?

I remember God showing me how the things I read distorted my belief in Him. When an author is guiding you to believe in the powers of the universe or in the deep powers of your sinful self without first leading you through the gateway of Jesus Christ, he aims to give you a false sense of empowerment and entitlement. Why glorify the creation and not the Creator? All that

> *If we need advice on how to truly live in our purpose, then we need to be advised by the one who created us, and further, the one who has offered to save us from death.*

we are, and have, has been gifted to us by our Saviour. If we need advice on how to truly live in our purpose, then we need to be advised by the one who created us, and further, the one who has offered to save us from death.

My taste in music changed over time as I could no longer listen to anything that did not contribute to my spiritual upliftment. I began to hate sin. I felt convicted every time I did wrong and even though I struggled with certain sins that had a stronghold on my life, God was patient and gracious with my imperfections.

I am a testament to the fact that God does not call the qualified. I want you to be assured that He qualifies those He calls. He loves chiselling and moulding those who are broken into persons that are wholesome and pleasing to His sight.

I grew up watching marriage with a "bad-eye" and I had absolutely no interest in its institution. However, I would learn that God does indeed have a sense of humour, because in June 2019 - I was walking down the aisle, getting married to a friend and business associate. Looking back now, I wonder if it was all a divine setup. Our relationship transitioned seamlessly from friendship into love. And just like that, I achieved a milestone I'd formerly despised.

My husband and I began going to church together, got re-baptized together and our lives have been undergoing a major transformation ever since. While we both have had very distinct journeys on this path, we share the common goal of seeking God until we find Him. God has been our ultimate source of provision and protection since we submitted our lives to His will and our lives have never been the same.

Shout out to my wonderful husband and family!

Like myself, it is my hope that my dear readers will take a baby step of faith and heed God's call. I know modern-day media urges us to take these big leaps of faith into our destiny, but no one reminds us of how powerful mustard seed faith can be. Mustard seed faith can move mountains, so why aren't the mountains in our lives being moved?

Ask yourself - have you ever truly believed? And who have you believed in, is it yourself, someone else, or God?

Sometimes we are unable to take big leaps of faith. But know that God will accept our baby steps of faith just the same. Faith is like a muscle. It needs to be conditioned, trained and given the right proteins to grow. When God invites us to come as we are with our imperfect and sin-laden selves, He is asking us to step into His realm of soul-building. God wants to transform our weaknesses into strengths, our baby steps into giant leaps, and move us from the shackles of death into an abundant life.

How then do we trust God without knowing where the journey with Him will take us here on earth? Ultimately, we know that with God we will spend our eternity with Him in our new eternal dwelling place; but how do we navigate life with Him in this temporal earthly realm?

We can have everything God's Word tells us we can have if only we BELIEVE! God has echoed this to me over and over again, causing me to take a good look at whether there was any evidence or testament of my belief. Think of Jesus Christ as the only eyeglasses through which you can see and understand yourself, God, and this world. Without Him, you are blind because of sin. Our carnal nature is designed and destined to cloud and distort our vision. When it comes to the promises of God, we will remain blind if we do not extinguish the blinders and infections that contaminate us and cause us not to see.

I am honoured to share with you the lessons that God has shared with me. I am just His messenger and God has willed me to show you how to navigate your life in the present, and for eternity, by cultivating your beliefs through God's Word. I pray that this book will be a blessing and a means for you to start taking baby steps into God's perfect will for your life.

You have already taken a baby step of faith by opening this book and availing yourself of God's revelations and insight. I pray that God's light will shine upon you as you read today!

CHAPTER

2

WHAT DO YOU BELIEVE ABOUT BELIEF?

Ephesians 1:18-19

"I pray that the eyes of your heart may be enlightened in order that you may know the hope to which He has called you, the riches of His glorious inheritance in His holy people, and His incomparably great power for us who believe."

We've been taught to believe in ourselves from a tender age, as we embarked on the path of socialization within our families, homes, schools, neighbourhoods, and churches. We use the word loosely as if it were a synonym for one's hope without assurance. Yet we are forever in a state of believing that we believe.

Britannica defines belief as "a mental attitude of acceptance or assent towards a proposition without the full intellectual knowledge required to guarantee its truth." It goes further to state that "belief becomes knowledge only when the truth of a proposition becomes evident to the believer."

By nature, however, the human heart is filled and overflowing with unbelief.

We love to gloat about getting to know ourselves and who we are through introspection, meditation and all sorts of fanciful universalistic practices. But if one is to truly know who they are, they must identify their first point of reference: their belief system. We are essentially what we believe, and our actions will always twist and turn in the direction of our convictions.

What shapes our convictions? Is it our parents, our culture, the teachings of the education system, our friends, the behaviours of our role models, etc? Or, is it the barrage of information overload we endure through social media? It is so easy to be convicted of a false narrative in this era of opinionists, false prophets, fact-checkers, media bloggers, influencers and attention seekers. But if our facts and opinions aren't curated according to the Word of God, we're in for some revelations and encounters that will humble our limited minds.

I want you to reflect on not just what you believe, but whose words you believe as well. Sometimes, we believe the assertions of persons whose minds have not been rooted in the Word of God. No matter their perceived high-rated intellectualism; anything not rooted in God's Word is not rooted in truth. We should therefore be careful of who we are listening to because words carry the power to infect or disinfect our souls.

If all things God are all things related to one's spirit, then I hope you know that it is erroneous to believe that spiritual truths can be intellectually perceived. A.W. Tozer wrote in his book *God's Pursuit of Man-* that "there is a kind of truth which can never be grasped by the intellect, for the intellect exists for the apprehension of ideas, and this truth consists not in ideas but in life. Divine truth is of the nature of spirit and for that reason can be received only by spiritual revelation."

We all have a deep yearning to believe ourselves and to believe in something. There is a difference between believing yourself and believing in yourself. One can easily believe the thoughts produced by their faulty mindset about themselves and others, without believing in the potential of their abilities and talents. Nonetheless, we all give priority to what we think over what others think, in both a positive and negative sense because we are innately biased creatures. Secondly, we all yearn to believe in a higher power, and we categorize and rationalize how we can access this innate or external power and place our hopes therein.

Some believe that this higher power is God, for some it is Allah, some place their trust in Norse Gods like Odin, and some simply accept that power can be sourced within the universe or nature. Many people believe that a higher power can be found within them. Essentially, we are all building singular hypotheses of faith based on our experiences, teachings, influences and circumstances.

Many believers claim to believe God, but their lives do not show any evidence of their so-called belief. There is no testimony of a greater power living within so many of us. If we truly believe in God and the truth of all that He has said, then why are so many Christians living powerless and defeated lives? How can you be the tail and not the head when you claim to have the Highest power of God resident within you? Could it be that you have falsely believed that God lives in your character but your behaviours prove that He does not? I hope you know that God doesn't live in you just because you say He does. Could it be that you have a false interpretation of who Jesus is? Have you crafted your own convenient version of Jesus in your mind? Or are you ignorant of the promises of God for those who believe in Him?

When life is going contrary to God's promises, we must stop and check our belief system. Do you keep driving when your vehicle is smoking and overheating? Do you not care about your internal engine? Have you believed in the fear tactics employed by the enemy instead of the restoring and powerful hand of God? Is your conviction skewed by your lack of understanding?

It is not enough to say you believe. We all have the freedom to say anything we desire. If you believe, you must then ACT in faith on that conviction. You say you believe in God, but you demand to see, hear and feel by way of your senses - as if God needs to prove His truth to you. You disregard God's sole requirement of faith because

> *It is not enough to say you believe. We all have the freedom to say anything we desire. If you believe, you must then Act in faith on that conviction.*

you assume it is better for God to show you a full picture of all that concerns you. As a matter of fact, we often believe in God when that belief shows instant benefits and makes us feel gratified. Do we dare believe in a God who doesn't show His hand or give us what we desire when it's convenient for us?

Do we really have to give up our freedom to partake in the things we love about the world if we say we believe? Can't we just get favour to manage our sins responsibly? *We're only human, right?!?*

Not too long ago, I remember taking advantage of God's grace. I would mumble at who God wanted me to be while pursuing who I wanted to be by the allowance of His grace. If He had all this power, then He had the ability to make me into whoever I desired to be. I remember trying to challenge God when I was younger, telling Him that I wanted Him to turn me into a singer. I clearly thought to myself that God was a genie and when I was not granted my wish, I had the authority to despise Him.

This is exactly why it is imperative that we have an accurate understanding of who God is and who we were created to be; not just for our enlightenment, but also for the spiritual illumination of generations to come.

How dare I think that my fallen self could instruct the God who created the Heavens and the earth, the God who formed man out of the dust of this earth, and the God who made us into living souls! How could I even begin to bargain with God when there was no consistency in my obedience, prayer life, worship, bible study, faith or tithing? I'd stopped honouring the House of God, promoting it as an option rather than presenting it as a necessity for worship, counsel and fellowship. It's no wonder I had no power, direction, or favour.

It isn't always a question of "Oh ye of little faith". Many times, it is a question of "Oh ye of little obedience".

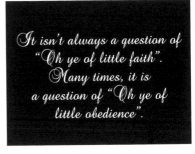

It isn't always a question of "Oh ye of little faith". Many times, it is a question of "Oh ye of little obedience".

The true Christian walk is supernatural and so faith demands that we cannot be governed by our senses, because our senses are governed by our flesh. We can have everything the Bible tells us we can have, but we cannot assume that we have it just because the Bible says so. Our beliefs about God, our identity, our health, and our relations must be based on spiritual truth and founded on God's spoken and written Word.

Our minds in their unrenewed states are always waging war against unbelief. Adam and Eve were exposed to all that God said was good and all that was pleasing in His sight in the Garden of Eden. They were not exposed to sin or death, yet the Devil was able to sow a seed of doubt. Imagine how it's even more tempting for us to be exposed to the attraction of sin. How easy it is for us to doubt God when we experience and observe sickness, death, poverty, and injustice in our daily lives.

How we live evidences what we believe about God. He doesn't force us to love Him. He doesn't even force us to believe Him. He calls us, compels us even, but ultimately it is our choice to believe that sin results in death and obeying His will results in eternal life. It is up to us to remove the blinders of unbelief and turn on the light switch in our hearts of darkness so that God can illuminate us from within.

I don't know why it's so easy for us to believe in everything, but God's Word. Our hearts are truly deceitful and wicked, as the Word says. We find ourselves talking faith with boldness, while secretly thinking doubt. We must develop the confidence to act on what we say. If we say we believe the Word of God, then it's high time we start acting like it.

Prayer:

Lord, I pray, that you would help us to believe in you and in the integrity of who you are. Help us believe when you speak a word that it will come to pass. Help us to not only believe but also to receive all that you have pronounced for us. Give us an encounter with your Word and renew our minds so that we can walk in Spirit and in Truth. Amen!

CONTEMPLATIONS

1. Who is God to you? Describe and explain who God is.

_____

_____

_____

_____

_____

2. Do you believe that your perspective on God and how He functions is accurate; OR do you believe there is a lot more for you to learn about the character of God?

_____

_____

_____

_____

_____

3. How much have you studied God's Word? Do you believe that you have to know His Word in order to know Him?

_____

_____

_____

_____

_____

4. Do you believe that sin is a big deal? Do you believe that a life, without God, will result in spiritual death (i.e. separation from God)?

_____

_____

_____

_____

_____

5. Do you believe that we can really walk by the spirit and live by faith or do you prefer living exclusively by way of your five senses?

_____

_____

_____

_____

_____

CHAPTER

3

THE FAMILY OF GOD

"Nothing compares with getting to know the God who knows us!" – David Jeremiah

"In the beginning was the Word, and the Word was with God, and the Word was God. He was with God in the beginning. Through Him all things were made; without Him nothing was made that has been made. In Him was life, and that life was the light of all mankind. The light shines in the darkness and the darkness has not overcome it." – John 1:1-5

$\mathcal{I}$n the book of John, "Word" is a translation of the Greek "logos" and represents Jesus Christ. Jesus Christ was, therefore:

- existent at the beginning of creation;
- with God;
- Himself – God as the 2nd person in the Trinity.

Jesus was therefore of the same eternal and infinite substance as God.

I mention who Jesus Christ is because we serve a Triune God of which Jesus is a divine part. He did not just exist from the time of His conception on earth. He has always been omnipresent. However, He manifested Himself as a man in human flesh to save us from the condemnation of death.

It is important that we study and show ourselves approved. We must not sit idly by assuming that attending church or watching sermons virtually is enough to spiritually feed us or activate the presence of God in our lives. It isn't! How can we believe in the dynamics of a divine being if we do not truly understand and get to know Him on a personal basis for ourselves?

God is a living, sovereign being. His essence cannot be captured in an idol conceived and fabricated by man's delusions. God laid the foundations of this earth and marked off its dimensions. He gives wisdom and understanding to those who please Him. It is He who changes times and seasons and sets up and removes kings. Who then is like our God? Mighty to save and the lover of our souls.

Your success or failure at having a relationship with God depends solely upon what you think of Him, and, even more-so, if you believe in Jesus Christ, His Son.

Your success or failure at having a relationship with God depends solely upon what you think of Him, and, even more-so, if you believe in Jesus Christ, His Son.

We invest time, money, and resources into getting to know our friends, co-workers, business partners, and family members. On social media, we follow the lives of persons we admire, and we read books and listen to podcasts of celebrities who inspire us. We grow accustomed to those we listen to often and become part of their communities, thus developing a sense of trust and belonging. When our favourite celebrities promote a product, person, or brand, we believe their assertions and accept that their recommendations are reliable and true.

When Arnold Schwarzenegger shows us a body building technique and outlines the results of his latest product, we don't question his credibility or investigate the technique shown, we simply follow it with the expectation that we will see results. When Kim Kardashian promotes a skin care line, we don't go investigating the properties and origin of the products, we simply take for granted that everything she says about the product is true. We take medicines without knowing or seeing what was put inside of them and believe that the diagnoses of the doctors are correct. We display acts of faith to the unknown everyday but when it comes to Jesus Christ, so many persons raise their eyebrows at His promises and are cautious of giving their allegiance to Him.

It seems as if allegiance to religion has maintained some measure of popularity throughout the ages. But we should be cautious because having a religion does not equate to having God. We would be wise not to fall as the Pharisees did because of spiritual blindness, ignorance, and unbelief.

People tend to question and contemplate their belief in Jesus Christ more than they question anything and anyone else. Some see God's sacrifice on the cross as just another Bible story, because their souls have not had the privilege of the Holy Spirit bearing witness to them.

> *People tend to question and contemplate their belief in Jesus Christ more than they question anything and anyone else.*

One of the reasons why I was inspired to write this book was because of the mounting levels of ignorance and unbelief within the Body of Christ. We often say we believe in God, but many of us do not truly know the God we claim to believe in - or serve. If you would like to challenge me, run a quick survey and ask some of your Christian acquaintances to tell you what they truly believe about Jesus Christ and if they have doubt about anything said in His Word.

Can you believe someone you've never met? Can you believe someone you have no relationship with?

I contemplated whether we have a hard time believing in God because of His intangible nature, but then I thought of all the celebrities we've never met, products we've never seen created, the thoughts we think but cannot see, the air we feel but cannot see or grasp, and the Wi-Fi connection we know is there but cannot touch. I don't know about you, but we seem to have grown quite accustomed to believing in the reality of many intangible things.

I proceeded to move along my thoughts, and I thought about when God did take on a tangible form. As the Son, He dressed in human flesh to become the Son of Man, to redeem mankind from their penalty of death. He took on this form – being born, chastised and subjected to death– and yet still, as He walked this earth, many did not believe He was the Messiah. Do you know what was even more alarming? It was the religious fraternity that did not believe and who promoted unbelief to others. Now that deserves a raised eyebrow!

Jesus Christ told them who He was, spoke the words of the Lord, told them who He was sent by, and proved Himself by displaying miracles and wonders and yet still many did not believe. *In John 4:48, Jesus told a certain royal official whose son was sick that "Unless you people see signs and wonders, you will never believe".* Jesus knew that He had to perform miracles to give unbelievers proof of who He said He was so that they might believe. While the miracles did strengthen the belief of the disciples and others, they did not prove effective for everyone. But do you know what is beautiful about this: - it wasn't supposed to.

John 6:36 reads "But as I told you, you have seen me and still you do not believe". When I think about how blindsided the Pharisees were by their religiosity, I cringe at how easy it is for us all to have the truth staring at us while being too self-righteous or super-intellectual to perceive it. Believers and unbelievers alike, if you

Believers and unbelievers alike, if you have been honoured with the esteemed opportunity to get to know Jesus Christ as your personal Lord and Saviour, count it as the most valuable gift you have ever been given.

have been honoured with the esteemed opportunity to get to know Jesus Christ as your personal Lord and Saviour, count it as the most valuable gift you have ever been given. If given the opportunity, please do not hesitate to unwrap that intangible gift in your heart. Remember, Jesus does not give to you as the world gives.

Being called out of the darkness is not a right, it is a privilege. I know some people may want to debate me on this one, but they will have to debate with the Word of God if they do. God does not call everyone into His kingdom. He surely did not waste His time trying to convince the Pharisees. Jesus has said that He knows His sheep and His sheep knows Him.

Let us explore some scriptures that affirm how set apart, prestigious, and chosen the children of God are:

John 5:21 – "For just as the Father raises the dead and gives them life, even so the Son gives life to whom He is pleased to give it."

John 6:37 – "All those the Father gives me will come to me, and whoever comes to me I will never drive away"

John 6:44 – "No one can come to me unless the Father who sent me draws them and I will raise them up at the last day"

John 6:65 – "This is why I told you that no one can come to me unless the Father has enabled them"

Our heirship into the family of God is conferred onto us. Jesus chooses us, draws us, and enables us to believe so that He can save us and give us life to overcome death and glorify Him. Those who are of this world cannot grasp this because they were not meant to. The world yearns to glorify self. The world seeks to normalize evil. The world masquerades evil intent as good. The world is self-ordaining, self-promoting and self-approving. The darkness is therefore unable to comprehend the Light because God has blinded their eyes and hardened their hearts.

John 8:47 says "Whoever belongs to God hears what God says. The reason you do not hear is that you do not belong to God."

By believing in Jesus Christ, we believe in the One who sent Him, and our belief and obedience guarantees us the promises of God. We get hyped up for job opportunities that come with great benefits or for investments with great returns. Meanwhile, all those benefits are superficial, short-lived, and barren. I want you to change your perspective by valuing the opportunity of salvation and the benefits that are truly life-giving, eternal, fruitful, and profitable.

Firstly, you should be hyped up for being called into the family of God – but I wonder if you know your rights as an heir of God and co-heir with Christ. Do you know the promises that have been bestowed unto you if you do live in obedience and not in darkness?

Maybe you have not been reading your Bible! Maybe the Pastor has never explicitly told you! It doesn't matter, because you are reading this book today for a reason and I expect you to take total advantage of the power of God inside of you and walk boldly into your purpose knowing that the darkness within you cannot overcome God's Light. You are in the world, but you are not of it and the God we serve has overcome the world. So darling, take heart.

It is very clear in the Scriptures that the work of God is to believe in the one He sent – Jesus Christ. While the Scriptures testify about God, we too must lead lives that can testify of His glory as well as witnesses. God requires that you believe in Jesus Christ in order to be saved. Now, it is not enough to say you believe and act contrary to that belief. You must carry that deep conviction within and honour and obey the God you claim to believe.

Additionally, God says that those who love Him obey His commands. This must be reiterated because many people think it's simply about reciting the sinner's prayer with no real evidence of transformation. Jesus says we can come as we are, but He does not expect us to stay as we are. There must be evidence of transformation

> *Jesus says we can come as we are, but He does not expect us to stay as we are. There must be evidence of transformation and illumination in God's chosen.*

and illumination in God's chosen.

Those who truly believe in Jesus Christ believe also in His words and in the words of those He has sent into the world, with guidance from the Holy Spirit, to spread the message of His Word. *John 13:20 reads "Very truly I tell you, whoever accepts anyone I send accepts me; and whoever accepts me accepts the one who sent me."*

While Jesus tasks His believers with spreading the message of His Word, it is essential that we understand that Jesus, alone, knows who His sheep are and who He will be calling into His family. He will be calling them out of this world, out of imperfection, out of a sin-laden and broken life. We therefore ought not to play God. We ought not to try to decide who is deserving and undeserving. We ought not to decide who deserves God's grace. We do not have the authority to condemn or judge, for not even Jesus came to condemn but rather He came to save. We are God's sheepfold, going in and out of His pasture. Our responsibility is to make the profound Word of God so widespread and impactful that it will alarm and fibrillate those who are called and chosen so they can seek God and find their way into the pasture through the gatekeeper Jesus Christ.

> We therefore ought not to play God. We ought not to try to decide who is deserving and undeserving. We ought not to decide who deserves God's grace.

Our lives should be expressions of the One who sent us. Our lives must manifest Scripture and serve as a testimony of the One who dwells within us. Our lives must be an expression of God's creative ideas and intentions. God will make a way for His message to be heard through apostles, prophets, teachers, preachers, actors, entrepreneurs, poets, painters, singers, dancers, cleaners, nurses, doctors, politicians. We are all God's messengers.

The journey of believing God and activating faith starts with revelation. I would therefore end this chapter by giving insight into some of the promises of God bestowed upon our lives as obedient believers:

- *Everyone who believes in Jesus Christ will have eternal life in Him – John 3:16*

- *Being born again allows us to see the Kingdom of God – John 3:3*

- *Rivers of living water will flow from inside of us – John 7:38*

- *We are not condemned and will not die in our sins – John 8:24*

- *We will know the truth because it will be revealed to us – John 8:32*

- *We will be set free from slavery to our sins, and we will become slaves of righteousness – Romans 6:18*

- *Jesus will open up our eyes from spiritual blindness – Acts 26:18*

- *Jesus will never drive us away or allow us to be snatched from His hands – John 10:28*

- *God has promised to honour those who serve Jesus Christ, His Son – John 12:26*

- *We will have the power to do great works as Jesus Christ did when he walked the earth and even greater works than these – John 14:12*

- *We can ask Jesus for anything in His name, and He will do it so that God will be glorified – John 14:13*

- *We are given the advocate to teach us, guide us with truth, help us, and be with us forever. The Advocate is the Holy Spirit, or the Spirit of Truth, who will live with us and be in us – John 14:26*

- *As friends of God, we are chosen to bear fruit that would last – John 15:16*

- *We are brought into complete unity as being one with Christ who is one with God – John 17:23*

Prayer:

I pray that God will give us understanding and that His promises will be made manifest in our lives. I thank God for adopting us into His family and for our inheritance as heirs. I pray that you would draw us closer to you and shower us with your blessings in season. Amen!

PONDER ON THIS!

If you do not study God's Word, you resign your life to ignorance and defeat. As a child of God, it is your responsibility to know and understand the context, principles, and promises of all that God has said in His Word. It's the only way for you to learn about God's character.

When a child is adopted into a family, on earth, he must adapt to the rules, instructions, norms, and practices of his new household. It is the same with God. When you are adopted into God's kingdom family as a co-heir with Christ, you must adapt and submit to God's regime.

Do you eat once a week? Can such an eating pattern sustain you? So why then do we avoid the daily sustenance of God's Word? That should be our daily bread. Going to church on a Sunday is not enough to feed your soul or grant you power over your circumstances. You must study to show yourself approved.

Why is communicating with God only seen as priority when we are in want or need of something? Would you share your trade secrets and resources with someone you have no relationship or investment with? Why, then, do we treat our relationship with God so haphazardly as if getting to know Him is burdensome?

Do you believe that you have put enough time and effort into knowing God and all that He has said, and continues to say?

CHAPTER

4

A CASE FOR BELIEVING
IN SALVATION (PT.1)

Romans 10: 9-10

"That if you confess with your mouth, "Jesus is Lord," and believe in your heart that God raised him from the dead, you will be saved. For it is with your heart that you believe and are justified, and it is with your mouth that you confess and are saved."

$\mathcal{S}$alvation is defined as the saving of the soul from sin, guilt, and the consequence of peril, by God. The soul houses the mind, will, emotions, and is the seat of our human consciousness. Would it surprise you if I said that a large fraction of church folk and unbelievers across the globe still do not have a true understanding of what salvation is and why it was offered to mankind? I believe the church has not done enough to explain why Jesus offered redemption through salvation to humanity and why we were not worthy of it.

Salvation does not mean running to God as an emotional response to a complicated or disastrous time in one's life. I have seen many persons run down on a pew on an emotional charge of wanting to change their circumstances but not so much their heart, mind, character, behaviour, or lifestyle. Salvation is also not an end-of-year resolution; where you envision change, but end up succumbing to the familiar.

Critics argue that if God is such a kind and forgiving God, why didn't He forgive Adam and Eve immediately after the great fall and reinstate them under His care and leadership in the garden. Why all this doom, gloom, and spiritual fanfare? After all, God had an option to abort His mission and start over humanity right there and then. What did He have to lose?

Well, maybe these critics do not see the value in the redemption of humanity. Had God aborted His mission, none of us would be here today. I don't know what kind of love this is that God would give us a second chance at a relationship with Him, but I am thankful. We cannot afford to have the world trivialize what Jesus did for us on the cross and so that is why I must put forward my case for us to believe in salvation.

There are two dimensions to this life; the spiritual and the earthly. The earthly is just a shadow of the spiritual for nothing can be established on earth (good or bad) unless it has been established in the spiritual realm. This is why Jesus instructs us to pray for God's will to be done on earth as it is in Heaven.

Keep up with me now!

The spiritual realm works with very definite and precise spiritual laws. One of the laws laid down is outlined in **Ezekiel 18:20, which reads "The soul that sinneth, it shall die".** Note that it does not specify colour, race, ethnicity, gender, age or any other descript. The penalty of death applies to all souls that sin, in perpetuity. These spiritual laws were made by God and are part of God's justice system. Therefore, when Adam and Eve sinned, they catapulted mankind into a tragedy of eternal proportions. God is not a man that He should lie. His words are forever and amen. So, God's integrity would not allow Him to go back on any of the laws He crafted and instituted to govern the spiritual and earthly realms.

Satan, the father of lies, was intentional and calculated in his ruse in the Garden of Eden. Knowing that God could not go back on His Word, Satan sought to put an end to man, whom God loved and had made in the image of Himself. After all, God had kicked Satan out of Heaven and created a perfect earth for man to have dominion over. No wonder the Devil was so injuriously jealous! The Devil sought to be glorified and wasn't. Then to add insult to the injury on his ego – God moved on to create man in His image and likeness to further glorify the sagacious power of God.

Pay close attention to how the deception of man was brought about through Satan's words. I implore you to be careful of who you are listening to because words have the power to sow doubt and fear or to enlighten and empower. Adam and Eve's disobedience had far reaching effects because their fall gave Satan power over death. It allowed Satan to pull the trigger and fire shots aimed at killing God's purpose in man.

I implore you to be careful of who you are listening to because words have the power to sow doubt and fear or to enlighten and empower.

The following points highlight some of what Satan may consider as his achievements in deceiving man and fuelling their disobedience. Satan attempted to overcome light with darkness and the ripple effects of man's fall enabled Satan:

- *To sow doubt and unbelief in God and in all that He said – Genesis 3:1*

- *To replicate disobedience on earth as Satan did in Heaven when he disobeyed God – Ezekiel 28:13-19 / Ephesians 2:1-2*

- *To have man lose his identity of God in him and assume the identity of Satan. Man was now enabled to reject light for darkness – John 3:19*

- *To destroy the relationship between God and man – Genesis 6:7 / Isaiah 59:1-2*

- *To render man spiritually dead – Romans 5:12/ Romans 6:23 / Romans 8:6*

- *To strip man of his delegated authority over the earth – Psalms 115:16 / Luke 4:5-7*

- *To make man ignorant and blinded to the truth – Ephesians 4:18 / Isaiah 56:10*

- *To make man unable to fully express the glory, holiness, and power of God through him as a vessel – 1 Corinthians 6:19-20 / 1 Corinthians 3:16-17*

- *To dirty God's temples in man with ungodliness – 2 Timothy 3:2-4 / Mark 7:20-23*

- *To destroy instant communication and communion with God – Isaiah 59:2 / John 9:31/ Job 35:12-13*

- *To lose the authority and power of man's words on everything God gave him dominion over – Leviticus 26:18-20 / Haggai 1:7-11*

If we are to understand what Jesus Christ came on earth to restore, we must understand all that Adam lost when he sinned. What was the significance of Jesus Christ's (both human and divine) coming as the second Adam to restore God's glory and relationship with man?

Before the fall, God had blessed Adam with the authority to be fruitful and multiply. After the fall, God did not curse Adam, for sin was already a curse all by itself. Rather than curse Adam, God cursed the ground (Genesis 3:17). **This meant that the earth, its atmosphere and elements were then given the right to resist man's dominion.**

Adam's fall brought death, degeneration, and corruption to the cosmos itself. As man fell, so too did the earth fall away from God's original intention. Man was no longer in alignment with God, and the earth became misaligned from the authority of man because we lost the weight and security of God's glory and power to back up our every word.

> *Adam's fall brought death, degeneration, and corruption to the cosmos itself. As man fell, so too did the earth fall away from God's original intention.*

Every time you see a natural disaster, let it be a sobering reminder of man's disobedience!

Isaiah 24: 4-6 reads:

**"The earth dries up and withers,
the world languishes and withers,
the Heavens languish with the earth.
The earth is defiled by its people;
they have disobeyed the laws,
violated the statutes and broken the everlasting covenant.
Therefore a curse consumes the earth;
its people must bear their guilt.
Therefore earth's inhabitants are burned up,
and very few are left.**

CONTEMPLATIONS

1. Did you ever believe your sins to be so injurious to yourself and your relationship with God?

_____

_____

_____

_____

_____

2. Have you learned anything new about salvation?

_____

_____

_____

_____

3. Do you agree with God's justice system or do you think it's unfair? Do you think you would have had the capability to earn salvation if that was possible or do you appreciate the fact that belief in Jesus is the only way to have eternal life?

_____

_____

_____

_____

_____

CHAPTER

5

A CASE FOR BELIEF
IN SALVATION(PT.2)

$\mathcal{S}$atan was busy digging a pit for God's integrity to fall into; as his very nature is to kill, steal and destroy. Once again, Satan proved to be no match for the God, who created all things and for whom all things were made. God's ways are higher than our ways and His thoughts are higher than our thoughts. And still, the ways and thoughts of the devil are far lower than His.

Hebrews 9:22 stated another integral law, one that would send the Devil and his plot down into his own pit. This scripture states, "The Law requires that nearly everything be cleansed with blood and without the shedding of blood there is no forgiveness."

In order to eradicate sin, there must be shedding of blood!

Every man born is born of blood. But because of the fall, every man is now born of sin and rendered unclean. An unclean man would not be able to shed his unclean blood to cleanse himself or others from sin. The shedding of blood must come from a vessel of human flesh that is sinless and must be born of God's spirit in order to conquer death.

Sin is like a bacterium that infects your blood and causes lethal sepsis. The only cure for that blood poisoning is Jesus Christ. He, alone, holds the power to break the curse of sin and death.

> *Sin is like a bacterium that infects your blood and causes lethal sepsis. The only cure for that blood poisoning is Jesus Christ.*

Satan may have thought that he was winning the battle, but he was not prepared for the war that God was about to unleash on him through His adoption of man to sonship. While sin came into the world by one man, so too did God orchestrate His plan of redemption through the actions of one man.

Romans 5:19 reads:

"For just as through the disobedience of the one man the many were made sinners, so also through the obedience of the one man the many will be made righteous."

Jesus, the Messiah, whom we call 'Yeshua Hamashiach,' offered us salvation – which essentially means he has offered to salvage our souls from the condemnation of death, if we choose to let Him. Jesus did not come to condemn us, but rather to save us: we were already condemned. When sin entered this world, we forfeited our right to govern the earth, we severed our relationship with God and we went into hiding. When God came and walked the earth, He used His time of evangelism not only to spread the gospel but also to show us God's original intent for our lives.

Man, by his very nature, cannot offer perfection to God and so man cannot win or earn his way to God by way of his works. Salvation is a gift from God. Hence, the reason why Jesus established a New Covenant of sonship through faith with us.

Romans 7:6 reads "But now, by dying to what once bound us, we have been released from the law (Old Covenant) so that we

serve in the new way of the Spirit and not in the old way of the written code."

Jesus is not interested in what we do: he is interested in who we become. Just as He became the Son of Man for our sake, we should become children of God for our sake. We are accepting our inheritance as co-heirs (with Christ)

> *Jesus is not interested in what we do: he is interested in who we become.*

for us, not for Him. God is God all by himself, so we are doing Him no favours. God needs nothing from us; He is mindful of us because He loves us. The love of God was made manifest among us when He sent His only begotten Son into the world so that we may live through Him.

Did you know that even the creation yearns for our revelation and salvation? The redemption that Christ has offered us has significant cosmic consequences. God did not just come to free mankind alone; He came to set the cosmos free as well. If God could restore man, man could then restore everything that was originally designed to be under his dominion.

Romans 8: 19-23 reads:

"For the creation waits in eager expectation for the children of God to be revealed. For the creation was subjected to frustration, not by its own choice, but by the will of the one who subjected it, in hope that the creation itself will be liberated from its bondage to decay and brought into the freedom and glory of the children of God.

We know that the whole creation has been groaning as in the pains of childbirth right up to the present time. Not only so, but we ourselves, who have the first fruits of the Spirit, groan inwardly as we wait eagerly for our adoption to sonship, the redemption of our bodies."

May we not only remember our disobedience when nature reacts in catastrophe and disaster but also the gracious redemption that the earth awaits.

Satan has beguiled our nations with dressed-up ignorance. Our identity as children of God has been lost because of spiritual blindness. So many of us are living powerless lives because we do not fully comprehend the price for our sins that was paid on the Cross. When God was conceived as a man by the Holy Spirit, this sealed the beginning of a new creation. So when we accept Jesus Christ as our Lord and Saviour, we are submitting ourselves to the will of God to become a new creature in Him. If we are indeed a new creation in God, we are now carriers of the true Higher Power.

We indeed are the true superheroes of this world!

We indeed are the true superheroes of this world!

Jesus Christ did not come to hand out access passes to Heaven. It is our right to receive the inheritance of citizenship in the Kingdom of God. Jesus Christ came to demonstrate God's power and glory. And just as God spoke creation into being at the beginning of time, so too were we originally designed to have power and authority through our words. The power of life and death has always rested in our mouths. It was always God's intention that we could speak to a mountain and move it with words of authority. Jesus walked the earth displaying miracles, signs, and wonders by the authority of God. He left with us His power to produce greater works than He did – according to His will.

When God created man, He made our flesh out of the dust of the earth. When God cursed Satan for deceiving His creation, He cursed the serpent to the ground to eat dust all his life. Have you ever thought about whether dust was symbolic for the enemy feeding off man's corrupted flesh? – Suppose that, God is beckoning you to be transfigured into a new creation so that the enemy can stop feeding on you. The enemy and his cohorts are hungry and are seeking satisfaction of their hunger and thirst by feeding off the carnal appetites and lusts of the flesh every time we indulge in them. Despite this, God has empowered us and given us the right and power to expose and starve the enemy because we are no longer confounded by the flesh.

Ephesians 5:11 reads

"Having nothing to do with the fruitless deeds of darkness, but rather expose them."

Do you know the coming of Jesus Christ broke down all barriers to the covenant of God's promise? Jews and Gentiles became one when Jesus set aside the law with its regulations and commands. Jesus created one humanity, with no division, which allowed everyone the opportunity to be reconciled – Jew and Gentile. We all have access to God by one spirit now. Everyone called into God's kingdom, through Jesus Christ, is a member of the same household, and citizens of the Kingdom of God.

> *Everyone called into God's kingdom, through Jesus Christ, is a member of the same household, and citizens of the Kingdom of God.*

If the Gentiles are heirs along with Israel – members of one body and sharers together in the promise of Christ – then why are we still encouraging divisiveness in the Body of Christ?

I remember wanting to check on my Israelite heritage and God didn't seem flattered at all by it. I bought select books related to the topic and I was not getting incitement from the Lord in my journey to prove who the true Israelites were. I'd grown quite annoyed at the many, white-washed versions of the Israelites and all the stories relating to God. I was also carrying around a bit of a grudge that the persons who created the content had purposefully side-lined black and other minority people from Bible stories for ages. If the true Israelites were indeed scattered all over the Earth, then why were the media only focusing on one subset of people?

One day, it dawned on me – with the prompting of the Holy Spirit – that I was falling victim to the same thing many content creators were guilty of. Everyone wants to make it more about themselves than about God. I was unable to read the books with the mind of God and so I stopped. My motives were impure because I was seeking to validate myself and gain the approval of man by being counted as a true Israelite.

God said: this is why so many of us miss our blessings when they are not packaged in the form we desire. What's more, Jesus Christ came and changed the scope of genealogy and lineage by removing the value

God said: this is why so many of us miss our blessings when they are not packaged in the form we desire.

from such identities as he gave us new identities as sons of God. Our heritage is not Israelite or Gentile, we are adopted as sons of God. Even if my physical bloodline went back to a true Israelite, it did not matter anymore in the spiritual realm and it was not profitable for me to become side-tracked in fact-checking when God needed me to focus my energies on soul-saving and His will. There are many persons who can attest to having an authentic Israelite bloodline, but who are not sons of God and vice versa.

Romans 2:28-29 reads:

"A person is not a Jew who is one only outwardly, nor is circumcision merely outward and physical. No, a person is a Jew who is one inwardly; and circumcision is circumcision of the heart, by the Spirit, not by the written code. Such a person's praise is not from other people but from God."

Not everything we may deem to be good is profitable. I have had to come to terms with this revelation over time. We all have our innate biases, opinions and preferences. That is why our relationship with God is so important: so that He can reel us back to the Word and the promptings of the Holy Spirit whenever our thoughts and beliefs go astray.

Your call to God's pasture was not of your doing. In the next chapter, you will learn that we don't find Jesus; it is Jesus who finds us. Next time you are praying for an unbeliever, pray that Jesus will draw him/her unto Him, because it is only God who can change and enable the hearts of man.

If only salvation was as simple a feat as a written exam, we would be able to regurgitate theories and practice for the practicum of such an exam. Salvation is given by grace through faith alone, not by works. If it were by works, the playing field would not be levelled. The rich would have an advantage over the poor. The educated would claim they had more intellect than the uneducated. The workaholic would work His way to the prize much faster than the slothful man. Salvation is available based on something we all have equally in common and for free: our belief.

We tend to focus our energies exclusively on the fight between good and evil and forget that the real fight consists of life versus death. Like Adam and Eve, we grapple with the tree of knowledge of good and evil which only seeks to produce a yardstick for good works. The true purpose of God's redemption, however, is to give us eternal life as he originally intended us to have.

We tend to focus our energies exclusively on the fight between good and evil and forget that the real fight consists of life versus death

This book is a message from the messenger, to a dispensation of believers, who God is seeking to equip and restore the original intent of His Glory within. God desires that when we speak, our words would have the power to defeat the enemy. We are the superheroes we admire. Actually, we are even greater because our power is backed up by the authority and force of God.

This book is a clarion call. It raises the alarm for God's army to start aggressively gathering as we move into a new territory of battle in our spiritual lives. God is seeking those who are eager for a true renewal of their nature as they put their old nature to death. God wants to offer us His gift of salvation and shine His light through the tunnels of our darkness so we can find our way home.

Prayer:

Lord, we thank you for your gift of salvation. We want the rivers of your living water to flow through us. Empower us with your armour, protection, and power to defeat the enemy as we take back control and dominion over the territories of our lives. Amen!

REFLECT ON THIS!

*Our aspiration should be to reflect
the ways and characteristics of God.
We ought to be rooted in Christ so we
can bear good fruit and have the dominion
God intended us to have.*

*If you allow God to have absolute dominion
over your mind and body, what do you think
your reflection will look like here on earth?*

*Do you believe that we are the true superheroes
on earth?*

CHAPTER

6

PURPOSE OF MAN AND
THE WAR WITHIN

Quote by A.W. Tozer:

"Pulled out of the mud of your own ego, so that you have stopped thinking that you are somebody, at last you are delivered from yourself and are seeking God for Himself alone."

Psalm 8: 3-8:

"When I consider Your Heavens, the work of Your fingers,
The moon and the stars, which You have ordained,
What is man that You are mindful of him,
And the son of man that You visit him?
For You have made him a little lower than the angels,
And You have crowned him with glory and honour.
You have made him to have dominion over the works of Your hands;
You have put all things under his feet,
All sheep and oxen—

Even the beasts of the field,
The birds of the air,
And the fish of the sea
That pass through the paths of the seas."

Our hearts have longed for a deep answer to this question since the beginning of time: What is the purpose of man?

Maybe Adam and Eve did not understand their purpose. They had everything, except the fruit of a tree, that belonged to God. Clearly, God knew that the knowledge of good and evil would be to the detriment of mankind. The world today continues to experience this detriment because we long to know and experience everything.

Many scientists and spiritualists alike have taken knowledge and twisted it to the delusions of their own self-willed grandeur. They manipulate good with evil motives, and they call evil good believing that life is within the power of their intellect. They disregard God's intentions and purposes for humanity. But of course, God endures and gives man over to the depravities of their minds.

Romans 1:28

Furthermore, just as they did not think it worthwhile to retain the knowledge of God, so God gave them over to a depraved mind, so that they do what ought not to be done.

The question remains, however, Why was man created?

God created the Earth and prepared it for man before He formed man in His own image. Formed for God's pleasure, He blessed man with gifts, talents, and abilities. He also took delight in intimate communion with him. Man would glorify God and enjoy His presence forever. Everything in the Garden of Eden was created for man to use and cultivate. The things on Earth were meant to be external, supportive, and subservient to man. Things were made to serve man, not the other way around. Within man was God, and he was given an organ by which he would know God and ascertain things of the spirit.

When man fell, the things on the Earth (and the gifts given to us) replaced God on the throne within our hearts. We longed to possess what we already had dominion over for fear of losing things in the same way we became lost to God. When Adam and Eve fell, they hid from God. Just as our earthly parents did, we also hide from Him in shame and find delight in the praises of our flesh. The further from God we move, the further we move from our purpose. While we may still carry around the embedded giftings, talents, and abilities God has blessed us with, our purposes are buried in who we glorify our giftings and opportunities with and how we use them.

1 Corinthians 12: 4-7

"There are different kinds of gifts, but the same Spirit distributes them. There are different kinds of service, but the same Lord. There are different kinds of working, but in all of them and in everyone it is the same God at work. Now to each one the manifestation of the Spirit is given for the common good."

Nothing belongs to us, not even our children. We are merely vessels and stewards used by God to make His investments in a person manifest. Everything was gifted to us for God's purpose, not for our own. God holds the individual manuals for our lives, but we have forsaken his manual for a bootleg version.

> *We are merely vessels and stewards used by God to make His investments in a person manifest. Everything was gifted to us for God's purpose, not for our own. God holds the individual manuals for our lives, but we have forsaken his manual for a bootleg version.*

Let's do an honest assessment of our hearts and minds. The first stage in redemption is admitting that we are nothing but a big lump of sin. We were all born sinners and in us dwelleth no good thing. While we may reveal our sinfulness differently, we were all born of the same pedigree of sin. It's a fact that we are all dark and void just as the Earth was before God said "Let there be light."

Now that we've got that covered, let us be honest about who or what rules us. Have we forced God out of the temple of our hearts and replaced Him with lovers, money, fame, religion, food, material things, our jobs and even the idolizing of our talents, physique, or beauty?

I know it's easy to treasure things of this world – especially the things about us that bring us acclamation – but nothing is safe that is not committed into God's hands for His purpose. May we place God unchallenged on the throne of our hearts, knowing that all that we are, and have, is by the allowance of God's grace.

We all have a specific calling and inheritance in God. Both the revelation and accomplishment of this requires that we walk in close relationship with the Holy Spirit, who is God with us. The Holy Spirit serves as our guide and teacher, and compels us to search for the deep things of God.

To find God, and the treasures of His purpose(s) for our lives, is the ultimate triumph of fulfilment one can ever hope to achieve in this earthly realm. All other pursuits will eventually be proven to be meaningless, vain, and empty because true satisfaction can only be found in God. We must ground our aspirations on both God's overarching plan for mankind and God's specific plan for our unique assignments on earth.

Our viewpoint of who God is must be correct before we can understand what we were created for. For a man to know God, he must give his time and attention to Him like anything else. While money may be the currency of this earth, there is a currency in the spiritual world, called, our attention. It is said that whatever controls our

> *Too often we approach God with lazy faith, self-centred intentions, and haphazard obedience.*

attention controls us. Too often we approach God with lazy faith, self-centred intentions, and haphazard obedience. We expect God to give us a quick fix to our sorrows and the cheat sheet to the exam of life.

I can't count how many times I have been guilty of neglecting spending time with God in favour of Netflix, work, exercise, sleep or downright laziness. What's interesting, though, is that as the world advances into a conglomerate of digitalized assets and attractions, we are seeing where the battle for the currency of our attention has taken off in the earthly realm as it has been in Heaven. We give attention to what we BELIEVE is valuable. Whatever you find yourself thinking about when you are free to think as you please says a lot about what you value.

I was tasked with writing this book for all of 2021, but I allowed my time to be consumed with work and family commitments. This book is a testament to God's grace, and second chances, because His promise that I would have this book draft written in 2021 was sure. After going through a miscarriage in November, I truly believe that God designed my downtime with Covid-19 to be used for an uptime with Him, and the purposes for which He needed this book created. So here I am, isolated in my room for three weeks in December 2021, in anticipation of a new year, and God is using me to do in three weeks what should have been done all year. I can assure you that whatever the Devil has crafted for evil, God will surely turn it around for His good.

We behave as if time with God is optional, and we often do not treat God with the seriousness that He deserves. Yet, we expect God to give us preferential treatment when we do decide to go to Him in prayer. We are bent on giving glory to everything but God, and social media has only worsened this propensity. So many young persons are aspiring to be influencers. But imagine having a platform where you promote yourself, your sexy body of dust and the works of your hands that were uniquely created by God – but you never use it to promote Jesus Christ.

Some persons put forward the defense that they do mention God on their platforms, but a mention is not a promotion. A mention is not an investment in leading people to the truth. Is it that you are ashamed of the One who knew you before He formed you in your mother's womb? We cannot manipulate God by mentioning or referencing Him. What does your life say about God? Is it truly an image of Him? Does it glorify Him? If not, you may have to reconsider the purpose or motive behind your mention of Him. God warned us to stay away from those who have a form of godliness but who deny the power of God within. He spoke to us in 2 Timothy about always being in a state of learning but never coming to the knowledge of truth. We can't remain in God's pre-school all our lives, knowing and reciting the alphabet of godliness without ever being able to take the written exam and do the practicum of God's truth.

Our time on earth begins and ends on God's accord and it is by His will that we are chosen out of many to be His few. We can no longer get away with knowing about God, **WE MUST GET TO KNOW HIM IN SPIRIT AND IN TRUTH.** The God we serve exists outside of the boundaries of time. Yet to know Him, we must give time to Him. This is the opportunity of time – the chance we have been given to get to know Him. This is our ultimate duty as believers amidst the many distractions competing for our time and interest in the world.

Knowing who we are, requires that we know God's original intent and purpose for our creation. Then we must unearth the complexities of our controversial natures and realise that God has given us the opportunity to be born again.

> *Knowing who we are, requires that we know God's original intent and purpose for our creation*

There is an active warzone at work within each of us, as our flesh and spirit are fiercely opposed to each other. – Because of this, there are days when we will win the fight in our spirit, but also days when we will lose the fight to our flesh.

The transition from an old creature to a new creature is not automatically given; rather, it is up to each individual person to make it happen. I can only tell you what God says about who you are when you are in darkness and who you are when you have crossed over to His light.

What do you believe about yourself as an unbeliever living in darkness? Do you believe that you are in control of your destiny if your destiny has already been condemned to death? Why would God desire to set you apart to become a new creature in His kingdom?

2 Corinthians 5:17 reads "Therefore, if anyone is in Christ, the new creation has come: The old has gone, the new is here!"

It is not the first time that God is working at filling a void of darkness. He did it when He created this world and commanded "let there be light." Now He is commanding it again in our lives:- "Let there be light in our catastrophe of darkness." God is still in the business of creating and working. Jesus Christ said ***"My Father is always at his work to this very day, and I too am working" in John 5:17.***

God longs to be close to man and He yearns for us to live in the intimacy of personal communion with Him. Since the fall, men have alienated themselves from God and hid from Him by devoting themselves and their passions to their own works and self-will. We focus heavily on finding love, finding happiness, getting an education, or a buzzing career, and developing our talents. Many times, these self-interests can become idols in our lives because we put the pursuit and accomplishment of them in front of our pursuit and accomplishment of living a Godly life and walking in God's purpose.

God's desire is not only to show us the promises He has in store for us, but rather, He wants to show us how we can have dominion over it. Before we can dominate and cultivate our land of purpose, opportunity or anointing, God must first prepare us. There is value in the process of preparation. He wants us to value the blessing of the land, but He doesn't want it to take precedence over our valuation of Him.

Imagine: life was perfect in the beginning, there was only good and God and yet man still chose to disobey.

Jesus came to do what the first Adam could not do, which was to remain obedient and faithful. Imagine: life was perfect in the beginning, there was only good and God and yet man still chose to disobey. God, in His wisdom, is now raising His elect to do good where there is a prevalence of evil. In the beginning, men had the freedom to choose their own master and they are once again given an opportunity to choose their master after being presented with the truth.

Which master will we choose to follow in the war we face within? We clamour for change in political regimes when we feel that an administration has not governed justly. How has your life been, living in the darkness? Do you think you deserve better governance of your body and spirit or are you satisfied stumbling in the dark? What benefit have you reaped from living in sin?

Romans 6:21

"What benefit did you reap at that time from the things you are now ashamed of? Those things result in death!"

There are many things posing as light, but they are not God's light. God has promised to do His part in taking care of us if we do our part in seeking the kingdom first. God desires that you become God-conscious not self-conscious. You are to focus on cultivating God in and through yourself by means of the inner workings of Jesus Christ. Our inward gaze must be shifted from self to God and when God finds us faithful, He will give us the power to transact business between Heaven and earth.

As you grow increasingly conscious of God, you will grow not only in knowledge but also in revelation. The only difference between the saved and the lost is our currency of faith and attention. God's Word has listed out the purposes of man from Genesis to Revelation and we must believe all that God has said.

The Purposes of Man (The New Creation):

- *To believe in Jesus Christ and the promises of God – 1 John 2:24-25 / 2 Peter 3:13 / Hebrews 10:36 / 2 Corinthians 1:20 / John 14:1-12*

- *To not waver in unbelief – Romans 4:20 / James 1:6-8 / Hebrews 10:23*

- *To grow in faith to do the works of God – Hebrews 6:1 /*

2 Thessalonians 1:3

- *To be holy – 2 Corinthians 7:1/ 1 Peter 1:15-16 / Hebrews 12:14*

- *To glorify God – 1 Corinthians 6:20 / 1 Corinthians 10:31/ John 15:8*

- *To become vessels for the Holy Spirit to abide in – 2 Corinthians 6:16 / 1 Corinthians 3:16-17 / 2 Timothy 1:14 / Romans 8:9*

- *To be the eternal dwelling place of God – Psalm 90:1*

- *To find rest in God – Matthew 11:28-30 / Isaiah 57:1-2 / Hebrews 4:10*

- *To be the bridge between Heaven and earth – 1 Corinthians 15:45-49 / Philippians 3:20-21*

- *To know God, understand His ways and fellowship with Him – 1 John 3:6 / Jeremiah 31:33-34 / Jeremiah 9:23-24 / Proverbs 4:7*

- *To please God and bring Him pleasure – Galatians 1:10 / 1 John 3:22 / 2 Corinthians 5:9 / Psalm 147:10-11 / Ephesians 5:8-10 / Psalm 149:4 / Ezekiel 18:32*

- *To know and do His will – John 7:17 / 1 John 2:17 / 1 Peter 4:2*

- *To worship God in spirit and in truth – John 4:23-24 / Philippians 3:3*

- *To be a witness and living testimony – 1 Timothy 6:12 / Acts 1:8 / Isaiah 43:10 / Acts 10:42*

- *To be God's messenger – 2 Corinthians 5:20 / Isaiah 6:8 / Malachi 2:7*

- *To die to sin – Romans 6:11 / Colossians 2:13 / Ephesians 2:1*

- *To bear good fruit – John 15:16 / Colossians 1:10 / Psalm 1:1-6*

- *To delight in God's law – Psalms 1:1-2 / Romans 7:22*

- *To be a slave to righteousness – Romans 6:15-23*

- *To live according to the Spirit of Christ and not the flesh – Galatians 5:16-25 / Romans 8:6-13*

- *To endure circumcision of the heart by the Spirit – Jeremiah 4:4 / Romans 2:29*

- *To develop our gifts and talents in alignment with God's purpose – Romans 12:6-8 / 1 Peter 4:10*

- *To be the salt of the earth – Matthew 5:13-16 / Mark 9:49-50*

We must know God not by hearsay. God has offered to do a new thing within us, but it is our response to His call and his inner work that matters. We should also be cautious of all that may stand in the way of our spiritual progress as we sojourn with Christ. What may hinder one may not hinder another and so we must always be watchful and discerning. The ultimate goal is for us to dwell with both the Spirit and the Truth, one should not be without the other.

God is the unbeginning One who is, and He created us and everything else. He, alone, is worthy of highlighting himself because He is self-caused! We are simply the effects of His cause. He is self-sustaining. We cannot sustain ourselves without Him. He is self-contained. We are self-depositing and withdrawing. When man dies, nothing in God dies, and He loses nothing while we lose everything that we stored up on earth.

Our bodies are the dwelling place for our spirits. They give our spirits a material existence and without the spirit, the body is dead. It is very alarming then, that we pay attention to life primarily from the materialistic perspective and ignore the superiority of our "spirit man". The mind is unfit for the task of knowing God; for our reason and intellect can only testify to what they know about God. To know God, however, is distinct from knowing about Him. One cannot know

God unless one has had an encounter of illumination in His spirit from above.

In the busyness of life, we forget that the results of our life in the flesh are a result of whatever is influencing us in the spirit. Because the flesh is hostile to God, we cannot accommodate the flesh when we are walking in the spirit. We must make it our duty to remind ourselves daily to walk through our physical life in the spirit ensuring that the Holy Spirit dwells within us, His secret place.

What then is man's purpose? To glorify God, to commune with God and to set his/her mind on what the Spirit desires.

Romans 8:5 reads "Those who live according to the flesh have their minds set on what the flesh desires; but those who live in accordance with the Spirit have their minds set on what the Spirit desires."

What then is man's purpose? To glorify God, to commune with God and to set his/her mind on what the Spirit desires.

Prayer:

Yahweh, we cry out to you today. As we wage war against our flesh, let your Holy Spirit come and take control. Stay on the throne of our hearts, Lord; and sound the alarm when a threat of the flesh is drawing nigh to the seat of our hearts. Let us walk in the delight of your purpose, not our own. We thank you for second chances and we bless your name. Amen!

CONTEMPLATIONS

WHAT DO YOU BELIEVE

1. Do you believe that you are a New Creation in Christ? Have you been born again? If not, why?

_____

_____

_____

_____

_____

2. I have listed out the purposes of mankind as a new creation in Christ. Which of these purposes have you been fulfilling? Which of these purposes do you need help and/or guidance for?

_____

_____

_____

_____

_____

3. Are you using your gifting and talents to glorify God? If not, why?

_____

_____

_____

_____

_____

4. Do you trust that God knows what is best for your life? Do you sometimes try to manipulate God to make your will into His will?

_____

_____

_____

_____

_____

CHAPTER

7

7

LOVE OR LUST

Someone recently wrote in ignorance on Facebook that "the God story" had too many missing pieces and they could not reasonably believe that God would kill His son instead of killing Satan. This critic made his assertions through the lens of the selfish nature of his flesh. He reasoned that if God is in fact God, He should be revengeful just like a human being would be and that it would be more practical to use his power to take out Satan instead of allowing His son to die.

There are so many things wrong with the mindset that pervades such thoughts. Firstly, this random person speaks like this because he does not know God nor does he know the character, nature, dispensations, or intentions of God. Further, he is ignorant of the reality of why God sent His son to die. He doesn't know that the reason the Son of God appeared was to destroy the Devil's work. God did not send Jesus to die to prove a point to Himself. Rather, He sent Jesus to die to save us (mankind) from His wrath. The power and nature of God were not reduced in any way after man's fall. It was man who became reduced from life to death. God's wrath is sure and promised for Satan, but He has offered humanity a way to escape His wrath because He loves man terribly.

It's imperative that we know God's Word for ourselves so that the cunning words of those who are ignorant would not sow seeds of doubt in our minds and lead our lives astray. Unfortunately, so many people believe that they can rationalize God, and His actions, based on the commonplace limitations of their intellect. Who are we to say what God should and should not do? Were we the ones that created the earth with the power of our words? Did we create the master plan for man, angels, animals, and trees? Did we separate light from darkness, or the land from the seas?

> *Who are we to say what God should and should not do? Were we the ones that created the earth with the power of our words?*

In Job 38, the Lord speaks to Job out of a storm and says "Who is this that obscures my plans with words without knowledge? Brace yourself like a man; I will question you and you shall answer me." He goes on to ask Job in chapter 40 "Will the one who contends with the Almighty correct him?"

We love to mask the haughty and hollow opinions of our minds, but the question is whether we can face being questioned by God. Do we really believe that our thoughts are more worthy of believing than the thoughts of God? If you desire to know how clueless, lowly, and foolish your thoughts are compared to God's, I would challenge you to try answering the questions posed by God to Job throughout chapters 38-41.

As clueless, ungrateful, disrespectful, unrighteous, and self-centred as we are, God loves us. God doesn't just profess that He loves us with His words, He proves it.

Romans 5:6-8

"You see, at just the right time, when we were still powerless, Christ died for the ungodly. Very rarely will anyone die for a righteous person, though for a good person someone might possibly dare to die. But God demonstrates his own love for us in this: While we were still sinners, Christ died for us."

God has proven His love for us on the cross and He continues to prove it by way of His grace every day. Even when humanity grieved God with the severity of their wickedness, God decided to reset us and not delete us.

> *Even when humanity grieved God with the severity of their wickedness, God decided to reset us and not delete us.*

I have been a lover of love ever since I wrote my first poem in Primary School. I always believed that it was something worthy of being found and I often wondered why it was so keen to elude me. I yearned to be loved and desired as the women in the movies and novels were, and I ignored all the tell-tale signs in my relationships which proved that I was experiencing lust not love.

Living life without God at the centre of your thoughts is in fact a dangerous thing. We are deceived to think that we are opening ourselves to love when in actuality we have opened ourselves to the lusts of the flesh. We don't see all that's lurking behind that door waiting for access. We open ourselves to sex and before you know it,we are stuck in a web and stronghold of pornography, masturbation, perversion, prostitution, heartbreak, revelry, abuse or frustration.

When we give in to the lusts of the flesh, we are really violating God's laws as mandated for the body. When we violate our bodies, we violate God because we are His image-bearers.

I remember struggling – like, really grappling– with masturbation and pornography as a young adult. It was such a struggle for me that I would sometimes have to force myself to sleep to ignore the temptation. Every time I did it, I felt hopelessly guilty and distant from God. Just like Adam and Eve, I would go into hiding and try to avoid God, as if His presence could be avoided. As I got closer to God, however, I could not bear the guilt and shame and my desires began shifting from pleasing myself to pleasing God. I knew God would not be pleased with me if I gave in to temptation. And bit by bit, God changed the desires of my heart and gave me the strength to overcome. Eventually, one day I woke up and I was free. I no longer had the cravings I once had.

God's love isn't the "butterflies in your stomach" type of love. It's also not a "love at first sight" type of love either. Naturally, we don't love God, nor do we want to love Him. We love the passions of our flesh because they are immediate, impulsive, reactive, and temporarily satisfying. Love comes from God, and it is God who loves us first. 1 John 4:19 reads "We love because he first loved us." It is only when we have had an encounter with God's love that we understand what true love really means. As we embrace God's love, our spirits yearn to please and obey Him, and we begin to wage war against our fleshly nature of sin. I promise you, though, that God is not waiting for you to be perfect before He can empower you to sin no more. As you are reborn of God, sin becomes less desirable. And while you are not perfect, God's grace will be sufficient to keep you in His light and perfect peace.

1 John 3:9

No one who is born of God will continue to sin, because God's seed remains in them; they cannot go on sinning, because they have been born of God."

So many of us work hard within our relationships to prove our love to our partners. We go over and beyond to exhibit that we are good husband and wife material. While this may not be the testimony of many in today's world, we see where people make wholehearted and half-hearted efforts to prove their worthiness to those they care deeply for. If we can be so intentional about our roles in our relationships, why aren't we intentional about how we treat God and please Him?

> *If we can be so intentional about our roles in our relationships, why aren't we intentional about how we treat God and please Him?*

Aren't we also in relationship and communion with our Abba Father? We grieved Him once before, are we intent on grieving Him again? Do we not value God's Word and believe that His commands are meant to keep us in perfect peace and victory? Don't we believe that He knows best for us because He made us and knows the plans that He has for us?

Human love is conditional, sometimes sporadic and very self-serving. It seeks to be reciprocated and that's why so many of us stay in abusive or toxic relationships. We think by staying we can prove ourselves, and our commitment, and earn some measure of reciprocity. Human love can be provisional, based upon a plethora of benefits. This is the new trend of love nowadays: we give love to get love, money, materialistic possessions, or even children in return. We say "for better or worse" in marriage, but when the worse shows up in a person, we recuse ourselves from our vows and disqualify our mate from being loved. Some love, simply to prove a point to themselves or to prove their worthiness to their family, rivals, or to their fans. There is always an "I" factor in humanistic love whether we like to admit it or not.

God legislates that we love Him, and the Bible explicitly tells us what defines love for God. *1 John 5:3-4 reads "In fact. This is love for God: to keep his commands. And his commands are not burdensome, for everyone born of God overcomes the world. This is the victory that has overcome the world, even our faith."*

There is no grey area or loophole in loving God. God measures our love by our obedience. You may be wondering what these commands are and if they are distinct from the ten commandments. These directives are not new, however, only reinforced.

If God is love and we do not love Him, is it safe to say that we do not love "love"? If we don't love "love", then what is this love that we keep professing to have for others? Is it love or lust that we have when we don't have God? Lust isn't only a sexual phenomenon. Many of us are ruled by passions that have nothing to do with sex. When the soul is undisciplined, it refuses to be satisfied with God and yields to cravings of any of the following three things:

- The lust of the flesh
- The lust of the eyes
- Pride of life

(Reference: 1 John 2:16)

God shows us the various elements of love through His commands, and He commands us as follows:

- *To not love the world or anything in the world – 1 John 2:15*
- *To believe in the name of God's Son, Jesus Christ – John 3:16 / John 6:47*
- *To love one another. To love our brothers and sisters – John 15:12-13*
- *To not continue to sin. To do what is right and be righteous – 1 John 5:18 / 1 John 3:9 / Deuteronomy 6:18 / Matthew 5:20*
- *To test the spirits to see whether they are from God or false prophets – 1 John 4:1-3 /*
- *To not love with words or speech but with actions and in truth – James 1:22-25 / Luke 6:46*

If we are image-bearers of God and God is love then we too must exemplify love. God's love is of a higher standard and so we aim to embody God's love, not humanistic love. – If we cannot love our neighbours who we can physically see, how can we love God who we cannot see?

If we are image-bearers of God and God is love then we too must exemplify love.

We can have all the riches of this world and great spiritual gifts such as prophecy and faith. But if we do not have love, we are nothing. The Bible doesn't say we have nothing, it says we are nothing. Truth be told, we really are nothing if we don't have God.

As for the critic I mentioned at the beginning of this chapter, I can only pray that God would reveal the truth unto him. People have been slandering what they do not understand for centuries.

Jude 1:10 reads "Yet these people slander whatever they do not understand, and the very things they do understand by instinct – as irrational animals do will destroy them."

When Adam and Eve disobeyed and opened their eyes to the knowledge of good and evil, they immediately became ignorant to the revelation of God. Remember: ignorance is a consequence of the flesh and the only way to counteract ignorance is with God's Spirit and truth. A man who speaks from his flesh will therefore never be able to understand the things of the Spirit.

While God's love abounds, His judgment abounds also. We should therefore not mischaracterize God's love as a passive, never-ending phenomenon of grace and a multitude of chances – while we purposefully deny His call to transformation and go on living in the darkness of sin.

While God's love abounds, His judgment abounds also.

Destruction and eternal fire are promised for those who do not believe. If you are a true believer, you will love God and obey. God would not command us to do something that He knows we cannot do. God knows we can love and obey Him with the help of the Holy Spirit, which He has promised to all those who believe.

Jude 1:5

"Though you already know all of this, I want to remind you that the Lord at one time delivered his people out of Egypt, but later destroyed those who did not believe."

PONDER ON THIS!

How many times have you gone over and beyond to love a spouse or a partner you were in relationship with?

How much time, will, and resources did you dedicate to that relationship?

How much compromise and forgiveness did you instil to keep your relationship afloat?

Have you ever given that same energy to knowing God and sustaining a relationship with Him?

Why is it so easy for us to compromise for a sinful man/woman but so difficult for us to submit to the love of a perfect God?

CHAPTER

8

PRACTICING SPIRITUAL AGRICULTURE

Jeremiah 17:7-8

But blessed is the man who trusts in the LORD, whose confidence is in Him. He is like a tree planted by the waters that sends out its roots toward the stream. It does not fear when the heat comes, and its leaves are always green. It does not worry in a year of drought, nor does it cease to produce fruit.

The God we serve is a Creator, a Cultivator, and a Saviour. He crafted the master-plan for everything He created, including us. When God created man, He created us as seeds, and we were designed to be planted and cultivated, to blossom and bear fruit. We were created to be splendours of glory for the Most High who reigns supreme over all the Earth. With beauty and purpose, we were meant to mature into trees that magnified the Lord.

In the beginning, God saw everything that He created and declared that it was good. Since the fall of man in the Garden of Eden, the seed of man has been sown in darkness. Like most seeds, we germinate in darkness because we are born of sin. Nonetheless, our Triune God (Father, Son and Holy Spirit) is there to provide us with everything we need to live from the time we have sprouted. He desires that we will live and not die. The Triune God provides us with a trinity of sunlight, water, and air to activate and sustain our growth.

We spend much of our youth as a seedling, urged by God to transplant and bury our roots into the Word of God. Ignorance usually permeates the air around this time and dampens us off from this call. Some heed God's call but many folks opt to root themselves in Satan's contaminated soil instead.

Our Triune God gives us all that we require to function as healthy, living organisms. God is the sunlight we need to photosynthesize – to create energy to grow, bloom, and produce seed. Jesus Christ, the Son, is the river of living water that carries the nutrients of God through us and causes us to bear fruit in season. The Holy Spirit, our guide, is the fresh air we need to respire and grow food to stay alive. Yes, it is critical that we have oxygen and find sustenance through the growth of our talents, work and giftings in order to stay alive and healthy.

We are TREES, just in case you are wondering. A human version, but a tree, nonetheless. Isn't it ironic that God gave Adam a garden to work in and cultivate as his primary assignment on Earth? I wonder if Adam did not realize that he was a tree himself. Both he and Eve were specially created trees, forbidden from partaking of a fruit that was not only contaminated but not of their kind. Adam and Eve had a choice to steer clear of the contaminated tree to avoid infection. They could have easily blossomed and taken root anywhere in the Garden with the luxury of having a constant source of sun, water and air. Remember: everything God created was good. God was pleased.

We do indeed take things for granted that are too easily available. We take the sunshine for granted because it is always there. Without fail or question, it shines morning after morning upon this world. Darkness has always been here, there, and everywhere. The world was void, dark and without form before God created the Earth. It is God who said, "Let there be light" and there was light. It is God who brought light into the atmosphere of darkness and the darkness comprehended it not. God brought light at the beginning of creation, and He is bringing it again to all those who seek to be a new creation. It really is that simple. To have eternal life and relationship with God, we must have light and it is God who gives light in the darkness.

As a new creation, we are reborn. We become rooted in the soil of God and not the soil of this diseased world. God gives us a built-in resistance to worldly diseases and pests such as greed, idolatry, sexual immorality, pride, and envy. When we are deeply rooted in the Word of God, the storms may come and some of our leaves may even fall. But our roots are so strong that our tree can be shaken, but never moved.

God wants us to know that we are safe and secure when we root in Him. Despite the darkness surrounding us, we can find warmth in His light, coolness in His river, and we can breathe in His air. We exist among a myriad of trees, some planted in the soil of the world, and some planted on God's Word. We need to focus on where our roots have been grounded as well as building our defences against the Devil who seeks to uproot and destroy us. He doesn't want us to be distracted by the other trees among us for even barren trees serve a purpose.

While we are rooted in the Spirit of God, we still exist in an environment that is pervaded by darkness and contamination. We become infected by diseases and destroyed by pests when we begin looking for sustenance outside of our Triune God. The sun is there, but we see other trees opting to go in the dark and receive artificial lighting because it seems intriguing and attractive. The Devil comes disguised as a brilliant modern age farmer who has charisma, and wit, about his smart farming. When we follow Him, we opt to be transplanted into soil or even water that promises to have greater benefits than our current circumstances.

> *While we are rooted in the Spirit of God, we still exist in an environment that is pervaded by darkness and contamination.*

We sometimes despise God's creative genius and are blind to how unique, yet symbiotic, He has made each of us. Tulips want to be roses and roses desire to be lilies and we lose sight of our unique DNA and God's intended purpose for our designs. If an orange tree cannot see the value in his oranges, the sweetness and health benefits, he will devalue his giftings; but should an orange tree forego its purpose and try being a mango tree?

> *Tulips want to be roses and roses desire to be lilies and we lose sight of our unique DNA and God's intended purpose for our designs.*

God wants us to know that we can only produce fruit of our own kind. We ought not to fight God's design. The longer the orange tree tries to be something he is not, the longer he will try bearing the wrong fruit in the wrong season. We must never forget that fruit is designed to be borne in season. God always has a season of preparation and a season of harvest. Are you trying to bear fruit when you should be preparing? Are you ready for a harvest or will your fruit fall to the ground to rot and waste?

> *God wants us to know that we can only produce fruit of our own kind.*

In Matthew 13, God shares a truth with us with the parable of the weeds. Good and evil people are allowed to grow together; but at the end of the world the righteous and unrighteous will be separated, as God weeds out everything that causes sin and does evil.

God's sunlight shines on everyone. It is available to the just and unjust, the innocent and guilty, the rich and the poor. The sun never stopped shining, the rivers haven't stopped flowing, and the breeze has not stopped blowing from the beginning of time to now. The unity of this trinity is not dependent on any sole person but on God's entire masterplan for man. It is we who choose to build ourselves greenhouses of unbelief that were never designed to produce fruit in man. The problem has never been the sun shining, it's us desiring to be shaded from our life source for a counterfeit plan.

The Devil is very cunning. He comes disguised as light. He will deceive you the same way he deceived Eve. Suddenly, he is asking you, "Did God really say you can't grow if you root yourself in worldly soil? He starts showing you how successful artificial lighting has become. He starts showing you hybrid plants and how thrilling the science of cross-pollination has become. You learn of all the benefits of existing in a controlled environment. You listen and it sounds logical, not spiritual. It sounds good but not God-like. And you eat from the tree again. You believe the words of a liar over the truth. You hide from God in shame when you learn that your tree is naked with withered leaves and no fruit.

Matthew 15:13 reads: "Every plant that my Heavenly Father has not planted will be rooted up."

Had you stayed rooted in God you would have found abundance. Where there is abundance there is provision because you are now able to share the bounty of your blessings and giftings with others. You may have taken in more sunlight than a young believer and may have more fruit. Your duty is to share it and inspire them to bask in sunlight more often. Your blessing is not just for you: your enlightenment empowers you to enlighten. When a tree is full in season, the earth cannot contain its harvest.

Your blessing is not just for you: your enlightenment empowers you to enlighten.

2 Corinthians 9:8

And God is able to bless you abundantly, so that in all things at all times, having all that you need, you will abound in every good work.

In the spirit, God has given us the right measure of each part of the trinity. He has even given us a greater light for the day and a lesser light for the night. God knows all that is needed for us to keep growing. In the beginning, God said "let there be light" and He is saying it again because light is the essence of life.

God gave Adam land (the Garden of Eden) to work and cultivate. But since man's fall, we have had to work on cultivating ourselves. Clearly, Adam did not understand his assignment. God is pleading with us to turn on His light in our souls. We all have an internal light switch; we just need to turn it on so that we can be illuminated in the darkness. The intensity of our darkness does not matter. Big sin, little sin or even what you may consider grey sin. Darkness is darkness. The problem is that we express our darkness in different ways, and so some people believe that their sins are dark but less dark than those of others.

God gave Adam land (the Garden of Eden) to work and cultivate. But since man's fall, we have had to work on cultivating ourselves.

Ephesians 5:8-11

"For you were once darkness, but now you are light in the Lord. Live as children of light (for the fruit of the light consists in all goodness, righteousness and truth) and find out what pleases the Lord. Have nothing to do with the fruitless deeds of darkness, but rather expose them."

God's ultimate desire is to illuminate you. He desires that you get to know Him and allow His trinity to nourish you so that you can blossom and bear fruit after your kind, in abundance and in season. No tree has lived forever on this earth. In this earthly realm, our trees have a finite life span, so I would encourage us not to waste our time here. We must number our days and respect times and seasons with understanding. We cannot afford to lose any more time being rooted in counterfeit plans.

Go to the master of your design and let Him direct you on the path to good fruit. Let us not waver in doubt. Let us not go to God half-heartedly. We cannot expect to grow if we are in darkness or contaminated soil. We cannot pick and choose and expose ourselves to moonlight but not sunlight. There is a reason why God has blessed the earth with both.

I can tell you the formula to greatness, to purpose, and eternal life. It is belief in Jesus. Come up hither and shine!

1 Corinthians 3:7

"So neither he who plants nor he who waters is anything, but only God who gives the growth"

REFLECT ON THIS!

Do you know what kind of tree you were created to be? If you can only produce fruit of your own kind, then look at what kind of fruit you have been producing.

How does God, our Father, reproduce Himself in us?

E.W. Kenyon wrote in His book titled "The Hidden Man: The New Self":

"There can be no development of the human spirit until it receives eternal life, in other words, until it is recreated. The New Birth has recreated this human spirit and imparted to it righteousness and the nature of God so that it can fellowship with God on terms of absolute equality. You may develop any gift that you wish to. The most important gift that God has given to you is the spirit. It is the development of this spirit that is going to mean more to your life than any other one thing.

The Holy Spirit recreates us through the Word. He imparts to us the nature of the Father, and with this impartation comes this new kind of Wisdom. Christ is made unto us Wisdom. This is accomplished when we are recreated. There is faith that will link us up with God, there is love that will make us God-like. There is stability that will make us as stable as God; and all the other wonderful attributes that have challenged us in the man Jesus, can be reproduced in us, as we walk in the light with Him."

CHAPTER

9

SOUL BUILDING FOR
THE KINGDOM WARRIOR

1 Samuel 16:7

"But the Lord said to Samuel, "Do not look on his appearance or on the height of his stature, because I have rejected him. For the Lord sees not as man sees: man looks on the outward appearance, but the Lord looks on the heart."

The Merriam Webster Dictionary defines body building as "the developing of the body through diet and exercise and specifically as the developing of the physique for competitive exhibition."

Our bodies have an unknown and limited lifespan and many of us find purpose in building our physiques for competition, leisure or "likes". This is commendable in the physical realm because it requires a huge amount of dedication and discipline to achieve one's desired look. However, body building focuses on self and the building and idolizing of one's body. If we can dedicate our time and character to developing such physical feats, we can also devote ourselves as Christians to the building up and maintenance of the physiques of our souls.

We are triune beings imaged after a Triune God. Our mortal trinity is made up of the body, soul and spirit. Within our souls lies another trinity: the mind, will and emotions. Our souls are the fabric of our character and that is why it is so critical that we focus more energies on the building of our souls than the building of our bodies. Though it's important to have both physical and spiritual health, I do believe that more emphasis needs to be placed on our spiritual health, as this affects not just our transient life but our eternal life as well.

Soul building is really about the building and strengthening of one's character. When you build your body, you show off how you look. But when you build your soul you show off who you are. If how I look is temporary and who I am is eternal, then I'd place more emphasis on the character from which I cannot escape.

Human beings are always in a state of becoming. We are always developing on the trajectories of good or evil, well-intentioned or not. Our spiritual evolution, or devolution, as individuals hinges upon the choices we make, the habits we create, the God-given assignments we complete and the beliefs we believe.

Our physical hearts are muscles and they operate more efficiently with exercise. So too do our inner hearts need spiritual exercise to operate with proficiency in this world. Our overarching aim is to build so much inner muscle and strength that our spiritual physique becomes a marvel

> *Our overarching aim is to build so much inner muscle and strength that our spiritual physique becomes a marvel of light to the world.*

of light to the world. Now that's attractive! If God is light, I would like to work out my heart and my mind until I have built enough muscle to begin glistening like Him.

Ever since I gave my life to Jesus, I have been attending the gym for God's divinity. Working out in the spirit can be more of a challenge than working out in the flesh. In the flesh, we have set times to hit the gym or to do our morning or evening runs. In the spirit, it feels like I am on that treadmill of faith all day, lifting the weights of prayer without ceasing and bench pressing my way through difficult seasons every single day.

When God gave me that ultimatum to cross over into salvation or lose His protection, I felt as if I'd just gone through a very traumatic rescue mission. I was confused, heartbroken, angry and on a continuum of making bad choices. God had to intervene to save me not only from myself, but ultimately from the penalty of death. Looking back now, I can absolutely cherish how God came into my burning building of sin and rescued me. When God rescues us though, He doesn't leave us shelter-less. He gives us refuge in the shelter of the Most High and offers to give us a new temple. God goes even further to teach us about our spiritual health, and He gives a lifetime membership in His gym to His elect.

Like every other programme, dream, or career in life, all novices and professionals must undergo some measure of training and development. It is no different in God's gym. Knowing and serving God is not for the slothful or the double-minded man. The more time and work you put in, the greater your results and the closer your relationship will be.

God offers us free lifelong membership but it's still our choice to get up every day and attend. Sometimes God will instruct you to meet Him at 5 o clock in the morning because He has carved out one-on-one training sessions with you in prayer and the study of His Word. It takes will, discipline, and commitment to achieve intimacy with the Holy Spirit and for His anointing to manifest in your life.

Both our self-motivation and external motivation wax and wane when we commit ourselves to a dream or task. Sometimes it's easier to have a gym partner because it's more fun when we have company and that way it's harder to quit. The church is the same. It's easier to build our souls when we have brothers and sisters in Christ who act as spotters to help us lift our heavy weights. We have qualified instructors who can teach and empower us about spiritual techniques and exercises like prayer and faith. Can you imagine a newbie in the Christian faith coming in and seeing that the diet required is to eat of Jesus's flesh and drink of His blood? We need guidance, support, and a network of like-minded persons to bond and grow with. In the end, we can all take the stage and show off our spiritual physiques and how good God has been to us through our testimonies.

Throughout history, God has always shown us spiritual realities through physical manifestations, and we should be discerning of this. We must stay spiritually fit and open to what God is saying and doing in every season. Off-season, pre-season, and in-season training are not just for professional athletes. We are all running a race in this realm. Some will have to run many different races, but God's conditions are all the same. God trains and instructs His soldiers with particular exercises to fulfil His purpose through different seasons:

- Season of preparation– PRAYER AND STUDY
- Season of strengthening and conditioning– FAITH
- Season of assignment or warfare – OBEDIENCE

These exercises are not exclusive to any one season as we are always in states of prayer, study, faith, and obedience. Additionally, these are not the only spiritual exercises one must practice. We go through different seasons in our lives based on our God-given assignment or state of affairs and we are required to turn it up a notch in particular spiritual exercises, based on the season we are in. The following three exercises serve as an example of mandatory exercises required by anyone who dares to submit to God's will.

PRAYER AND STUDY

We all start as amateurs in prayer. Actually, God has indicated that we do not know the right way to pray in Romans 8:26-28 and so He has sent His Holy Spirit to act as our interpreter and messenger.

Talking to God can sometimes feel like a burdensome task amid all our priorities, commitments, and distractions. If we are honest, our prayer life is usually at its strongest when our lives need a fire escape from an impending or immediate disaster. Disaster comes in all forms, from grief to joblessness, to broken-heartedness. While Christ has promised to be a very present help in trouble, He expects us to live our lives in constant communion with Him. The sum total of our acts and thoughts dedicated to Him should be our prayers.

Our prayers are like transactions within the Heavenly realm. God is in the business of giving, receiving, crediting, and refunding prayers in the prayer bank of Heaven. The answers to our prayers are sometimes immediate. At other times, they are stored up to be received later, at a time that is the most equipped for God's larger plan.

> *Our prayers are like transactions within the Heavenly realm. God is in the business of giving, receiving, crediting, and refunding prayers in the prayer bank of Heaven.*

Prayers are the daily stretches we do before and after we study God's Word and throughout the day. Scholars say that the more regularly you stretch, the better it is for the body, and your circulation. Did you know that stretching plays a critical role in body building because it is important for flexibility, rapid muscle growth, coordination, and most importantly the prevention of injury?

As we are preparing for our God-given assignment or for spiritual warfare, we must increase our daily output of prayer so that we may have divine direction and intervention. During this period, we should invest our time heavily in reading God's word and fasting. Our prayers also act as defences against the perils of injury caused by sin. We are stretching in prayer to armour ourselves against the impending arrows of sin that are directed against us daily. Sins such as idolatry, pride, greed, perversion and disobedience are trying to distract us and get us off our divine course every day. We must pray and read our Bibles to feed and sustain our souls consistently.

We are not praying to God for Him to alter the journey that is our pre-established destiny. We are praying for Him to give us direction to tread the path with wisdom, holiness, faith, boldness, courage, and protection because we know there will be treasures stored up at the end.

Psalm 91:15

He shall call upon me, and I will answer him: I will be with him in trouble; I will deliver him and honour him.

In the book titled "Prayer: Communing with God in Everything", A.W. Tozer expounds on his insight: "It is important that we keep in mind that God will not alter His eternal purposes at the word of a man. We do not pray in order to persuade God to change His mind. Prayer is not an assault upon the reluctance of God, nor an effort to secure a suspension of His will for us or for those for whom we pray. Prayer is not intended to overcome God and "move His arm." God will never be other than Himself, no matter how many people pray, nor how long, nor how earnestly."

The prayer stretches that we do are not for God. They are for us. God has no need to stretch. We are stretching for our own spiritual health, direction, and protection. Stretching can be erroneous, inconvenient, and one of those tasks that we rush through when we just want to get to the main event. If we don't stretch properly, however, we risk being wounded on the field; and once we're wounded, the game is over for us. For some of us, this means we have delayed receiving our trophy. For some, it means we have lost the fight and are sent into a season of recovery and preparation for a journey we should have already completed. For some, a wound may result in death signalling the end of one's destiny on earth.

At this stage in my life, I do feel compelled to complete my God-given assignments and win my battles, even as I acquire a few battle scars throughout my short time on this earth. Once we are alive, we have no choice but to keep moving; but the question remains, "Where are we traversing to?" I don't want to look back on my life and see that I wasted it traversing aimlessly on every path, except the one God planned on directing me on. The truth is we keep going down paths that weren't designed for us. God's hand of protection and reconciliation will not

> *"I don't want to look back on my life and see that I wasted it traversing aimlessly on every path, except the one God planned on directing me on.*

be on every path, especially when we are purposefully disobeying.

FAITH

For a believer, faith is not optional. It's a command. Because it's a command from our chief commander, Jesus Christ, we hold on to scriptures like *John 21:22 which reads: "If you believe, you will receive whatever you ask for in prayer."* We have faith that if we believe, we will receive.

According to Hebrews 11:1, faith is the assurance or guarantee of things we hope for and the conviction of things we cannot see. This means that we hope for things that we cannot see. We cannot see God's overall plan, but we have hope that the plan is for our good, and we trust that this is true. I believe we have more difficulty trusting God with our individual plans. We can accept the overarching goal of salvation for mankind, but can we accept God's offer to salvage our soul and His training arrangement for our transformation?

Imagine that we are in God's divine fitness programme. We're in between the divine gym and the field. We're ready to go to the next level. We've been praying, reading our bibles, and fasting. Maybe we're expecting a job promotion or maybe God promised us that the time for our Boaz was near. Whatever it is, we have hope that we will receive it even though we cannot see who, or where, our blessing is.

God tells you it's time for high-intensity training and you ask Him to at least show you your training plan and even a blueprint of who you're destined to become. At least if you know the plan, you can better prepare yourself for the training and maybe even do it for yourself on some days. You can even make some suggestions because your opinion should have some validity too, when it comes to you.

God, in His wisdom, opts not to show you His entire plan, but He expects that you will turn up for training everyday and follow His instructions without question.

God, in His wisdom, opts not to show you His entire plan, but He expects that you will turn up for training everyday and follow His instructions without question. On some days, He may give you a heads up, a prophecy, or a revelation for the week ahead but you are to be dependent on Him. Ultimately, there are those who will oblige and others who will surely rebel; but whatever one chooses to do, God still holds our plans in His hands.

When we realise how volatile human nature is, I believe- it would be better for us to leave our plans in God's hands. What difference is it going to make if He shows you your entire life? Your humanity will be inclined to question it, derail it, or make changes. There's a reason why God did not want Adam and Eve to know about good and evil. There is a divine power in trusting and not knowing.

Faith functions at its best when we don't know the trail for our assignment or purpose from beginning to end. Faith also functions best when the Holy Spirit is our GPS. The Holy Spirit serves as the navigator of our direction and tells us when to turn right or left. He warns of impending traffic and redirects our path when there is an obstacle or blockage in the way.

One must grow the muscle of faith with endurance and the cardiovascular exercising of one's hope. We do not need to know everything; we need to know God. As parents, we use wisdom in knowing what to disclose to our kids based on their age and maturity. Do you think God would be a responsible father if He told us everything we desired to know? How many times have you made a bad decision by knowing and not understanding, or jumping to conclusions too quickly? Sometimes, we must journey through the unknown to get to our purpose so that we develop the mass of trust within our muscles of faith. Trust adds bulk to our spiritual physique. It is evidence to God, and others, that we have been spiritually exercising and our muscles are growing.

It's important that while you are building up yourself that you do not fall victim to idolizing yourself. You've built some spiritual mass and you're sexy and glowing with the blessings of having faith. This is what happened with Satan when he was Lucifer. He looked at himself, his position, his beauty and power, and believed that he should be God. Sometimes, God keeps us dependent to humble us. Can you imagine knowing that God is going to bless you with that promotion next week Tuesday? Suddenly, you're going to work with your head held high. You begin making changes around your office and there is a decline in your consultations and training with God. Naturally, you are thankful, but you are anxious for Tuesday to come. The promotion becomes your focus, and you stop being invested in the path you are yet to complete with God.

At the end of each journey, there is a blessing. But before the end, there is always a lesson. Don't jump off the trail before you complete it. The lesson is oftentimes very close to the finish line. Further to this, we are always in need of direction. Completion of one path simply means we're at the beginning of another so that's why our reliance must be on God continually and not on things.

OBEDIENCE

Where there is faith, there is obedience, for one cannot know God's will if one does not obey. Obedience is how we breathe. We are living, breathing souls and we ought to live our every breath in obedience to God.

Genesis 2:7

"Then the LORD God formed a man from the dust of the ground and breathed into his nostrils the breath of life, and the man became a living being."

The way in which we inhale and exhale our words and thoughts matters. What we breathe into our minds is what we breathe out through our words. Our pattern and rhythm of breathing affects how well we function when completing the spiritual assignments and techniques given to us.

We feed our physical muscles with our breathing. We can similarly feed our faith in a posture of prayer with our obedience. Everything is intimately connected in our bodies; from our blood vessels, to our muscles, to our organs. It is the same with our souls – our mind, will, and emotions are all connected and affected by our obedience. On the physical level, this may look like obeying the doctor's orders. On the spiritual level, we are to follow God's orders and His prescriptions that result in the fruits of the spirit.

James 1:22

"Do not merely listen to the word, and so deceive yourselves. Do what it says."

Nothing pleases God more than seeing us walk by faith. Sometimes, God requires that we perform some very strange and uncommon acts to prove our obedience to Him. Personally, I think the stranger it is, the greater the reward; though possibly even the greater the ridicule from the world. When God tells you to walk around your Jericho seven times, you better ignore all the onlookers who jeer with their opinions of ignorance and blow your trumpet.

> Nothing pleases God more than seeing us walk by faith.

Noah walked with God and displayed unwavering obedience to Him when he was instructed to build the ark. Noah did not question why God wanted the ark built to His specific dimensions. Noah was faithful and obedient in a world where everyone else was disobedient and sinful.

There is a great reward in breathing obedience. Every breath we take should be a breath of God. We can't physically see our breath when we're breathing but it's evident that we have the breath of life. We can't see or touch our thoughts when we're thinking but our thoughts carry the invisible wind of belief or unbelief into our minds. We can't see our words when we're speaking, but we can see them when they are written down. And within them, they hold the power of death and life.

CONTEMPLATIONS

1. Do you take a disciplined approach to staying fit and eating healthy? How important is physical health to you?

_____

_____

_____

_____

_____

2. How much of an effort do you make to stay spiritually healthy? Do you take your spiritual health seriously? If not, why?

_____

_____

_____

_____

_____

3. What areas of spiritual health are you weak in? (Faith, Obedience, Prayer, or Study of the Word)

_____

_____

_____

_____

_____

4. Are you guilty of only praying steadfastly when you are either in trouble or in want of a desire? How do you intend on improving your prayer life?

_____

_____

_____

_____

_____

5. Do you believe that children should obey and respect their parents? Why?

    As a child of God, rate yourself on a scale of 1-10 on how obedient and respectful of God and His Word you have been?

_____

_____

_____

_____

_____

CHAPTER

10

THE POWER OF WORDS

$\mathcal{G}$od used words to create the Heavens and the earth. He then used words to create mankind, for He said "Let us make mankind in our image, in our likeness…" He created mankind in the image of God as both male and female and He blessed them and said "Be fruitful and increase in number; fill the earth and subdue it…"

All of God's words are spoken in order to bring His intentions into effect. God did not just wander around in thought. He spoke His thoughts into being. It's interesting that God made these declarations for mankind before He formed man from the dust and breathed the breath of life into him to make him a living being. I infer, then, that when God made mankind and blessed them in His image, He was making them in the likeness and image of His spirit. When God formed man from the dust, it was to form a body that would act as the vessel and/or temple for the spirit of mankind, which was likened after God. How powerful!

God declared His words to the spirit of man, not to his body. When you speak to yourself and to others, where do you think your words would then take effect?

Words carry an indispensable power to create. They can create things, circumstances, character, purpose, destinies, life, death, and even sickness. Words are powerful tools that direct and control us because words are what we believe or disbelieve.

> *God declared His words to the spirit of man, not to his body. When you speak to yourself and to others, where do you think your words would then take effect?*

> *Words carry an indispensable power to create.*

If we study the life of Jesus when He walked the earth, we see how intentional He was when speaking God's words.

John 12:49

"For I did not speak on my own, but the Father who sent me commanded me to say all that I have spoken."

John 14:10

"Don't you believe that I am in the Father and the Father is in me? The words I speak are not my own, but my Father who lives in me does his work through me."

God's words stand supreme. God spoke His words through His son, Jesus Christ and He desires to speak His words through us as well. He desires to direct our tongues because whatever we speak must manifest itself. God advises that we hide His Word in our hearts because it is the only safe and accessible haven for it to live so that we do not live a life enslaved to sin.

Our hearts and our minds are inextricably linked as one. They are one just as the Father is one with the Son. When we keep God's Word in our hearts, we automatically keep it in our thoughts. Our thoughts shape our actions and our own words. Our actions and our words shape our reality and our destiny.

It's amazing that it's not how we look that shapes us; it's the intangible and secretive substance of our thoughts that determines who we are. Yet, we focus so much more of our energies on achieving bodily perfection rather than the perfecting of our thoughts.

> *It's amazing that it's not how we look that shapes us; it's the intangible and secretive substance of our thoughts that determines who we are.*

1 Corinthians 2:11

"For who knows a person's thoughts except their own spirit within them? In the same way no one knows the thoughts of God except the Spirit of God."

Psalms 139: 1-4

"You have searched me, LORD,
*   and you know me.*

You know when I sit and when I rise;
*   you perceive my thoughts from afar.*

You discern my going out and my lying down;
*   you are familiar with all my ways.*

Before a word is on my tongue
*   you, LORD, know it completely."*

Only your spirit, and God, know your thoughts. Not even the devil has access to them. The only thing you have within the purview of your control is your thoughts: the thoughts you have towards God, yourself, and others.

God may have planned an assignment for your life; an assignment that bears good fruit and prosperity, that would erase your current broken circumstance. God's plan can be forfeited, however, based on the words you speak. Because God does His will

> *Because God does His will through us, we have the power to get in His way, and ultimately our own way, through the words we speak and give life to.*

through us, we have the power to get in His way, and ultimately our own way, through the words we speak and give life to.

God's Word gives life, but the Devil's utterances speak death. If God is speaking healing into your infirmities, you must believe in your heart and confess with your mouth that you are healed. You do not recite that your infirmity is hopeless. As a child of God, you have the authority to speak life into your circumstance.

Words reveal what you are in agreement with. Once they are spoken or written, they are made manifest as a seed sown. Once a seed is sown, it will sprout in the right conditions. If you sow words of God's purpose in your life, they will bloom if your mind has the spiritual conditions of God's truth, faith, obedience, and belief. If you sow words of envy and bitterness, they will manifest if your mind has the conditions of sin.

> *Words reveal what you are in agreement with. Once they are spoken or written, they are made manifest as a seed sown. Once a seed is sown, it will sprout in the right conditions.*

The question that should bear heavy on you before you speak or write is: Who am I in agreement with? You are not decreeing your own mind, but the mind of God and the mind of God is His Word.

Are you in agreement with God's Word? Are you in agreement with what God has said to you? Are you in agreement with what the world says? Are you in agreement with the mental utterances of your flesh? Is the person you are agreeing with in agreement with God?

For anything to function in your life, you have to agree with it. If you do not agree with the words spoken by and written of God, then you are in disagreement.

1 Corinthians 2:14

"The natural person does not accept the things of the Spirit of God, for they are folly to him, and he is not able to understand

them because they are spiritually discerned."

2 Timothy 3:16

"All Scripture is breathed out by God and profitable for teaching, for reproof, for correction, and for training in righteousness."

Satan's nature is deceitful. He parades around the earth masking his evil motives and doings as light. Persons who live in darkness always think that their darkness is light because they have never seen the glory of God's light. They do not know what true light entails. A man-made light bulb cannot illuminate the world like the sun that God created and yet God's radiance is multitudinous and jillions of times brighter than the sun.

Satan creates situations, circumstances, conditions, and even thoughts that speak against what God is doing or about to do in your life. God will promise you that your breakthrough in a muddy circumstance is near and Satan will peddle thoughts asking you if that is what God really said. Satan seeks to have you doubt God, question Him, and even curse Him. This is what Satan sought to have Job do to God because he was blameless.

In the Bible, God urges us to guard our hearts and to be transformed by the renewing of our minds. Our thoughts remain unmanifested until we write, do, or say what we think. God has given us the invisible passageway of our thoughts to communicate with Him in secret. Through this passage way we can ask for the cleansing of our minds before anything is established on Earth.

I often liken sin to dust. Dust appears everywhere blowing in from the known and unknown. If we do not clean our houses daily, dust will accumulate. Sin is like that; it blows in from every direction. Its distractions are everywhere, and thanks to the global interconnectivity of the internet and social media we have become more exposed to the Sahara dust of sin that blows through far and wide, reaching all corners of the earth.

Even when we are busy doing good, evil thoughts appear. The problem comes when we agree with the thought and establish it as a written or spoken word or even act upon it. Social media have propelled a trend of asserting one's opinions with authority. Many times, the words thrust on the pages of people's timelines have not been authorized by God in one's mind. Imagine the number of things we have all manifested in our lives by way of our baseless written opinions. Many times, people can be found spewing divisiveness, self-centeredness and pride on their pages under the cloak of words that God said. People pick and choose scripture to ordain their opinions. Meanwhile, their lives and their minds have never seen the transformation of God.

James 1:26

If anyone thinks he is religious and does not bridle his tongue but deceives his heart, this person's religion is worthless.

Whatever we write or say is established and whatever is established is agreed with. What we agree with is given the authority to be made manifest in the world. How many of us seek God's advice and authorization before posting on social media? What we post is a direct reflection of what we think and what we think is a direct reflection of who we are. What would Jesus post? Do our postings bring glory to God in any way? Do our postings lead people to Christ? Are we interested in making our point or God's point? When people look at our profiles, do they see God through us?

We cannot allow ourselves to be overtaken with doing what seems "good" if it is not in alignment with doing "God". We cannot be overwhelmed by the boosting of our image on social media in order to gain "likes" and feed our superiority complex. In the end, did we focus on boosting the image of God within us, or did we focus on boosting the image of self? It is not our opinion that matters, it is God's opinion that takes precedence over all.

There is usually a huge disconnect between how we speak about God and how we speak about others who were made in His image. We need to be careful, not only of what we say about ourselves, but also what we say about others. Woe to those who can be found spewing ill-will towards a child of God! And while we are all made in God's image, none of us knows who has been identified as an heir in the family of God. Who knows the appointed time of one's transformation from darkness into the light? Therefore, let us not think too highly of ourselves and be found guilty of passing judgment on others. We do not know who is in God's promise and we can also be found guilty of stumbling in the darkness. We all stumble differently in the dark, but the same darkness of sin pervades us all.

James 3:2

"For we all stumble in many ways. And if anyone does not stumble in what he says, he is a perfect man, able also to bridle his whole body."

Romans 2:1

You, therefore, have no excuse, you who pass judgment on someone else, for at whatever point you judge another, you are condemning yourself, because you who pass judgment do the same things.

James 4:12

There is only one lawgiver and judge, he who is able to save and to destroy. But who are you to judge your neighbour?

When one recites to themselves and others that they are not beautiful, or not satisfied with the body God has crafted for their spirit, one establishes one's words and agrees with them. They may even be moved to enhance their bodies, bleach their skin, or do plastic surgery. They have acted on the belief that was established in their mind. They seek acceptance based on what the world has said is beautiful. Such a person did not agree with God when he said everything He made was good. For many, God's physical rendering of them was not good enough and so they chose to do something transformative about it.

On the other hand, God has said that no good thing dwelleth in us. He has said that sin has contaminated the good image that He made. He has shown us how sin will ultimately lead to our demise and death. He has offered to give us a transformation. He has given us safe passage to eternal life. If only we agree with Him, we will be a new creature in Christ. We will shine a light like no other and our radiance will illuminate the glory of God. God has shown us the glitches of physical transformation without spiritual transformation, yet many of us choose to ignore the plight of our souls.

We downplay how urgent and glistening the transformation of God is. It doesn't seem trendy, it's unpopular, and can even seem boring and unattractive compared to the sexy appeal of the world. So many do not desire to look like God. In their minds, His image is too dull compared to the images perpetuated by this world. They see no instant benefits or gratification in looking like God. In their minds, God can wait. In their hearts, they believe they can transform their souls themselves. They can do "good" while looking "good". People will use the time God has allotted them, spending the money they've earned (by God's grace) from the abilities God gave them (by His choosing), to look like what the Devil has told them is glorious. They do not seek to look like God, they want to be the gods of their own inner world. Just like Satan, they seek to glorify the self and not their Creator.

I know this may seem harsh. It does not mean that one's pursuit to change or enhance one's body is a sin in itself, or worth the condemnation of hell. I, too, have some areas of my body that I feel could look better with some contouring and enhancing by the world's standards. However, not everything good is profitable and not everything good is God. At the end of it all, God shall weigh our motives. The motive for one is not the motive for all. We must assess why we are urgently pursuing physical enhancement and not spiritual enhancement.

God cannot be pleased if one gives no time to Him, no tithe to His house for its furtherance, no heeding of His instructions, no obedience, no faith,— and yet they give money, time, resources ,and compliance to the world's idea of how they should look. Is it that you have believed what the world has said, but you haven't believed what God has said and promised to you? Is it that you have prioritized looking as the world promotes rather than looking like the image of God?

We need to be focused on looking like God! We need to be focused on seeking Him first! Our souls take priority over our bodies! Let us work at perfecting those first. Maybe, while we are working on our hearts and minds, we will encounter a different perspective on how we look. Who knows!!! We can invest time, money, and resources into getting to know God and why He created us the way He did. And when we do this, we can speak words of life, beauty, purpose, and transcendence into ourselves and others.

Our words have the power to hurt, or heal. Our actions show whose words we agree with in every aspect of our lives and God weighs the motives of our hearts. Being spiritually minded does not come naturally to our flesh. Our flesh and spirit are incessantly at war. It is the counsel of God that produces good thoughts and plans. While we are busy planning our lives and every action, remember that it is God who ultimately has the final say in your life, not the world.

Proverbs 16:1-2

"To humans belong the plans of the heart, but from the LORD comes the proper answer of the tongue. All a person's ways seem pure to them,but motives are weighed by the LORD."

The Book of John is profound in that it tells us a lot about how God communicates. God engineered us to speak His language but we can only do so in Spirit and Truth. Our flesh can only speak the languages of this world. As such, we are compelled to communicate with God in spirit.

God engineered us to speak His language but we can only do so in Spirit and Truth.

John 6:63

"It is the Spirit who gives life; the flesh is no help at all. The words that I have spoken to you are spirit and life."

To speak God's language, one must hear and understand it.

John 6:45

"It is written in the Prophets: 'They will all be taught by God.'[a] Everyone who has heard the Father and learned from him comes to me."

John 8:47

"Whoever is of God hears the words of God. The reason why you do not hear them is that you are not of God."

John 10:27

"My sheep hear my voice, and I know them, and they follow me."

Language should not be solely perceived of as a noun or an abstract thing that we allude to for reference. The spoken language is a verb, it's something that we do actively, in our thoughts and speech. We act on all that is communicated through language because it is language that steers our beliefs.

As the world advances, we see where language has begun shifting its prominence from physical to virtual realities. Facebook has rebranded itself as the Metaverse and so they will institute their own unique language and means of communicating based on what they value and believe.

When the descendants of Noah spoke one language, they agreed to build the Tower of Babel in the land of Shinar in Babylon. Just like it was for Lucifer, pride had settled in their hearts and they wanted to be just like God. They did not want to be holy like God, they wanted to establish themselves as mightier and smarter than He. If they could reach the Heavens for themselves, by their own will and accord, then maybe they would not need God. This story actually reminds me of the many structures we have been determined to build for ourselves in our careers, relationships, jobs, etc... so that we can be successful on our own accord, proving that we do not need God.

When God saw the pride and arrogance of the people, He did what only God can do. He established a sudden multiplicity of languages so they could no longer communicate and work together. That is how significant language is. If we are not of one language, we cannot agree. If we are not in agreement, we cannot build. Think about it – If we did not understand the language of Facebook, we would not be able to collectively agree with the terms of its use and how we communicate with one another via posts, tags, messages, etc. If we did not all agree that this platform was user friendly and communicable, then Facebook would not have had a platform to build upon. There would be no Metaverse today.

When we hear God's language, we should be compelled to learn it and speak it. If you are from an English-speaking territory and you decide to move to Venezuela, you have to learn Spanish. It is the same with the Kingdom:- to enter it you must learn God's language.

After hearing God's language through His Word and His Spirt, we must be doers of all that we hear. *James 1:22 reads "But be doers of the word, and not hearers only, deceiving yourselves."* We must not deceive ourselves into thinking that our hearing automatically qualifies our calling or choosing. We must believe that God's language supersedes all forms of man's language and live our lives based upon its communication.

To speak God's language, one must:

- *Believe in the Triune God – John 10:30 / 1 John 5:6-8 / John 14:9-11*

- *Speak and activate faith, not fear! – Matthew 21:22 / Isaiah 55:11 / Mark 11:23 / Psalm 34:4*

- *Speak words that are connected to that which is eternal, not temporal – Matthew 12:36-37 / Proverbs 18:4 / Proverbs 30:32*

- *Speak in agreement with what God has said and not in opposition to His Word – John 6:68 / Jeremiah 29:11 / Deuteronomy 28:1-14 / Matthew 18:19*

With a world population of over 7 Billion, we want to be in agreement with the only thing that has never changed, evolved, or fallen apart – the Word of God. We want to speak God's language and be remembered by Him.

While the industrialization of the world advances and technologies evolve, we must speak God's language throughout the different dispensations and generational trajectories. God has His sheep in every generation. We ought not to get complacent or irrelevant but rather, to understand man's language of the day. God's kingdom is diverse but His Spirit remains the same. From beginning to end, praises shall be in the mouth of His sheep. His language is constant and never-changing. And so in the Spirit, it is His Word we must keep.

CHAPTER

11

MY CLOSING DEFENCE
FOR A BELIEF IN GOD

Apostle Joshua Selman said:

"The law is that everything that follows you is the report card to what you believe. The signs shall follow them that believe. The way to drive out what is following you is not to tell it go away but to change what you believe."

> *"The law is that everything that follows you is the report card to what you believe.*

Whatever is following you is following your mindset because it has been mandated to honour that mindset.

As we peruse through the gospels of the New Testament, we see where Jesus instructed many of the persons He healed to "go thy way and sin no more". This is significant because Jesus is urging the men and women to stay cleansed and avoid bringing calamity upon themselves from any further contamination. Interestingly, we are now living through the global Covid-19 pandemic and we are urged to practice

145

handwashing and sanitizing frequently throughout the day. We can model this behaviour spiritually as a reminder to sin no more after we have received salvation and to live in a constant state of cleansing and renewal of our minds.

I urge you, my dear reader, to open your heart and believe in the words of God. You are not called to believe in what you said or what acclaimed philosophers have said, but rather, in what God has said. We commit ourselves to the advancement of our intellect by way of education and training. We mindlessly scroll through social media agreeing and disagreeing with the opinions of men. How much more valuable is one's spiritualization? Why aren't we preparing for life eternal by studying and obeying the Word of God?

When Jesus walked the earth, He spoke the words of His Father, not the words of Himself. He was intentional about what came out of His mouth. When one has control of their tongue, they have control over their entire body. So if we are to be like Jesus, we should be working towards controlling our tongues and speaking the words given to us by God.

For every stage of growth in our spiritual maturity, there is a different language and different revelations from the Holy Spirit. We must understand God's language and enter into agreement with the words spoken by Him and written through the conduit of the Holy Ghost. If faith is the only conqueror for fear, then we must come into agreement with faith, not works.

> If faith is the only conqueror for fear, then we must come into agreement with faith, not works.

We are living in an era in which irreligion and unbelief are trending. The counterculture of this world is filled with high and mighty criticism of God's Word, which people chop up, discount, and deride to their own demise. For many, there seems to be a disconnect between who we say God is and the reality of our everyday lives. Naturally, one's scepticism will grow when the supernatural and reality seem to be a far-fetched match. People must see the reality of God in their lives but this can only happen when they become one with God. – If your life is showing no evidence of the Shekinah of Jesus, there is something you do not know about him.

Knowing God will only be irrelevant and ungratifying for those who have set their eyes upon themselves or upon the carnality of another man. Those who believe that intellectual prowess, talents, business acumen, material possessions, bodily appearances, and religiosity can take them to the highest version of themselves are blind to the futility of such pursuits when weighed on a scale of eternity. No matter what we may consider as the heights of worldly greatness, if you don't have your eyes set upon God, you are only just a fool. A rich fool, a poor fool, a bootylicious fool, a humble fool, an educated fool, a career driven fool, a talented fool, a charitable fool – but a fool nonetheless.

Matthew 7:26

"And everyone who hears these words of mine and does not do them will be like a foolish man who built his house on the sand."

Proverbs 17:24

"The discerning sets his face toward wisdom, but the eyes of a fool are on the ends of the earth."

Proverbs 28:26

"Whoever trusts in his own mind is a fool, but he who walks in wisdom will be delivered."

I believe there are spiritual realities that manifest themselves physically as proof of our insight. For every spiritual reality, there is a physical manifestation. Before Adam and Eve sinned, they were naked but unaware of what nakedness was. As soon as they had natural knowledge of the humanistic morality of good and evil, they ran for cover and hid.

Sin will always seek to cover you with its limited version of morality and knowledge, causing you to ignore and scoff at the limitless version of knowledge and wisdom from God. The Tree of Knowledge of Good and Evil was forbidden because once we partake of it, our central focus becomes attached to "self". Our beliefs turn away from Christ who is the source of eternal life and shifts towards the dirtied morale of fallen mortals.

God placed two trees in the middle of the Garden: The Tree of Life and the Tree of Knowledge of Good and Evil. Adam and Eve could have eaten from the Tree of Life, but rather they chose to doubt God and eat of the Tree which God told them would specifically lead to death. Since the beginning of time, we have been choosing death over life. We choose the taskmasters of our desires over God time and time again.

We choose the taskmasters of our desires over God time and time again.

Knowing the Bible is not the ultimate goal of one's life: it is knowing the Triune God of the Book. The Bible should not unseat our relationship with God but rather enhance and support it. – The Bible should not become an idol, inspiring us to rituals and works to get brownie points to Heaven. God has already told us that it is only by faith and belief that we can enter through His gates. Our good works should naturally follow suit to our beliefs so we should never attempt to put the cart before the horse as if we can manipulate God.

God creates, knows, sees, fashions, teaches, crafts, allows, tears down and builds up. God permits, judges, silences, gives, takes, honours, blesses, punishes, avenges, helps, leads, protects, and forgives. May we seek to believe Jesus and follow Him. May we take heart in those who have gone before us – like Noah, Job, and Enoch – and know that it is possible to walk upright before the Lord. Let our faith supersede our doubt and let belief surpass our fears. Let God reign over our desires and His light brighten every dark room in our lives.

Psalm 94:8-11

"Take notice, you senseless ones among the people;

you fools, when will you become wise?
Does he who fashioned the ear not hear?
Does he who fashioned the eye not see?
Does he who disciplines nations not punish?
Does he who teaches mankind lack knowledge?
The Lord knows all human plans, he knows that they are
futile."

We are all parts of the total sum of God's imagination and creation!

Unbelief rears its ugly head in disagreement with that. Unbelief wants you to believe that all that God has said and promised to you is not true. It wants you to doubt and question if God really made you, loves you, and cares for you. Unbelief wants you to think that Adam and Eve were merely characters in a superficial story because it's illogical to think that humanity was damned by the eating of fruit. Unbelief wants you to believe in logic and science while questioning God's truth.

Unbelief seeks to question how knowledge of good and evil can be a bad thing. Unbelief wants you to think that your good is good enough to enter Heaven's gates. Unbelief questions the authenticity of God's love when bad things frequently happen to good people in this world. It never tells you that none of us are good except by God's grace because sin is a defiler regardless of the type. It never asks you "by whose standards are you good – yours or God's?"

Unbelief will cause you to have your own interpretations of God's Word. Unbelief will tell you it's only necessary to believe in oneself. Unbelief will tell you that you are the master of your destiny, forgetting to tell you one's ultimate destiny is not possessions but life or death. Unbelief will tell you it's okay to follow some, and not all, of God's instructions. Unbelief will have you believe that the Holy Spirit is your intuition or the universe calling.

Unbelief will tell you there is no God and that you are the subject of your own creation and evolution. Unbelief will tell you God can be understood and reasoned based on science and that with God there should never be mysticism. Unbelief will tell you to say you were ordained by God even though you've never submitted to God's will. Unbelief will tell you your will is God's will and God only desires that you be happy and not holy in this life.

Unbelief will cause you to question if that is what God really said. Like Eve, you will question the validity of God's Word. Unbelief will cause you to scoff at those who choose to believe because your sinful blinders cannot comprehend the spirit of God's Word. Unbelief will influence you into proving the point that you don't need to be a part of the Body of Christ in order to know God. Unbelief seeks to isolate you from the family of God. Unbelief doesn't want you to be accountable, encouraged, or guided by those who were appointed by God.

Unbelief doesn't want you to build a spiritual resume of the fruits of the spirit. Rather, it tells you to focus on building the works of the flesh. Unbelief wants you to make no contributions to the Body of Christ, only to the world, a focus which leads to hell. Unbelief will make you think that having God means you should have the nobility of being poor. Unbelief does not tell you that all God's sheep are blessed to go forth in abundance, not only on Earth but with the treasures they've stored up in Heaven as well. Unbelief will have you believe that physical exercise takes precedence over spiritual exercise as if your body will live forever and not pass away.

Unbelief is simply one's disagreement with the words of God.

> *Unbelief is simply one's disagreement with the words of God.*

Believing in Jesus Christ may seem to be too easy a route for the hard-hearted. Some people think that there are many other ways to God. Some even believe that, there are many other gods. The whole idea of having faith in Jesus Christ may seem superfluous, uneducated, unrealistic, illogical, and unscientific to many. They prefer to take a chance on what man can see and interpret to their own vain ends. What sucks, however, is that we are all promised an end to our meaningless toil here on earth. What then? What is your status when the same God you don't believe in clocks your time on Earth?

We were all given a specific timeframe to be alive on this Earth in our bodily form. I believe when death strikes, it means that the time and seasons allotted to our God-given purpose have run out. When that time comes, we would have either done one of three things:

- Fulfilled our God-given purpose(s)
- Fulfilled our self-driven purpose(s)
- Wasted our time

What did you choose to believe during your time? What did you build based upon your beliefs?

As I looked at the movie "Don't Look Up", starring Leonardo Di Caprio, I could not help but consider how self-preserving we are. The biggest and brightest nations have dedicated time, resources, money, and intellectual efforts to many forms of preserving humanity on earth and further preserving the resources that have huge financial value. Never before have we been so intentional about preserving the fallen state of man, and the earthly possessions we have attributed worth to.

Science and innovation have made so many radical advancements that many have fixed their gaze on it and further away from God. It's almost as if we have forgotten that it is God who has bestowed us with such knowledge in the first place. We think we are wise, but it is God who allows us to be wise in our own eyes. It's almost as if we seek to challenge the credibility of God when we tell others to put their trust in science and fact finding instead of in God.

The truth is that many would prefer if there was no God because they see no issue with their sins. They want to preserve the sinful state of man at all costs because they no longer see sin as sin. They want mankind to evolve through science as if science could uproot the seed of sin that was sown into man since the beginning of time. They long to preserve who they are and what they consider to be the highest version of themselves without any consultation with God. I would go further to say:- they want to contest God and create a new man after their own image.

They don't care about preserving their souls for God. Rather, they long to preserve their bodies for selfish gain and appeal. They think their smartness and inventions can appease God; as if God will ever be impressed with the limited and foolish actions of man's flesh. God feeds into the ignorance of many and purposefully lets the blind think that they are the ones who can see.

What we know and think we have discovered is only a miniscule element in God's entire plan for man. We shall be held accountable for the knowledge we sought and how we shared and manipulated it for our own selfish gain. If nothing was done to glorify God in Spirit and in truth, it shall be put to shame. If nothing we do connects to an eternal purpose, it is useless.

A man cannot be a man unless he has a spirit and a soul. He can create bodily structures, but it is God who breathes life into the cellular structure of a body. It is God who gives life and who takes it away. In the end... just like Lucifer, Adam and Eve, and the Tower of Babel, all of man's efforts to not need God and override His will shall end in shame.

> *In the end... just like Lucifer, Adam and Eve, and the Tower of Babel, all of man's efforts to not need God and override His will shall end in shame.*

We live in a dispensation where we only desire a connection with God when we are being blessed, but we eschew anything related to holiness. We desire to be blessed, but unholy, purposeful but not judged. We want to be morally "good", the better part of the two-sided tree. But like Adam and Eve, we ignore the other tree standing there because the image of God seems less gratifying for us as flesh bearers. 'Good' is subjective and seems flashy on the outside but God alone sees and knows the motives that lie beneath the surface of our flesh. Science will advance from now until eternity and still never know what's truly in a man's heart.

> *We desire to be blessed, but unholy, purposeful but not judged.*

I want us to really dig deep and ask ourselves: What are our beliefs about God and all that He has said? Why is it so hard to trust Him? Through the good times and the rough times, God has set out a roadmap for our lives. He never said our lives would be perfect in our fallen state. Once we are in this mortal vessel of flesh, we will always be at war with our spirit, but we need to trust that God has our back. We must believe in the roadmap provided because He is the only way to everlasting life. When we say life, we don't mean immortality. After our bodies die, our souls will live forever with either God or Satan. If God is life, then Satan can only be death. True death. True darkness. True hopelessness. True separation.

Without God, our spirit is dead to Christ. A dead man has no purpose, no intention, no continuity. Do we really want to give up life eternal for the pleasures of temporal humanity?

Connect yourself to eternity, and establish a purpose that connects you as a passerby on Earth to your inheritance as an heir in God's kingdom.

Sin separates us from God. The further away we feel from God, the closer we are to a lie the enemy has sown deceptively into our minds. Let's look at some subtle lies we entertain and believe from Satan:

1. When God says, "don't fornicate" – We say, "we have to taste the pot before we take it off the stove."

2. When God says, "seek Him first and all things will be added" – We say, "seek a career first and follow your own path and your blessings will be added."

3. When God says, "control your tongue" – We say, "we are free to speak our minds and be outspoken."

4. When God says, "love your enemies" – We say, "it is only wise to love ourselves and those who love us."

5. When God says, "the only way to Him is through salvation" – We say, "there must be another way."

6. When God says, "do not have a lying tongue" – We say,

"our white lies are intended for good not for evil."

7.   When God says, "wives submit to your husbands" – We
forget that God expects the man to first submit to God.

These are all signs of unbelief. When you create an alternative to God's Word, and make God into an option, you are telling God you know better than He does for yourself and mankind.

> When you create an alternative to God's Word, and make God into an option, you are telling God you know better than He does for yourself and mankind.

What have you not believed from God? What rules have you bent? Have you been playing hop scotch on both sides of the fence?

Life is everlasting in the spirit, not in the flesh. Our purposes and assignments must be connected to eternity, not to our carnality; carnality is temporal, which means it is only concerned with the present life in this world. Carnality is tied to earthly seasons, and is concerned only with what you can see, feel, hear, smell, and touch right now.

We have a responsibility to advance the kingdom of God on earth.

How do we begin to bear the things of Heaven on earth if we have no connection to the source of life? Without Jesus, you are operating on battery power because you are hooked to a temporary source of carnal life. Aren't you tired of changing batteries and jump-starting your life over and over in your flesh?

> How do we begin to bear the things of Heaven on earth if we have no connection to the source of life?

Unbelief drains energy from your battery quickly with sickness, doubt, ingratitude, joblessness, debt, hopelessness, infertility, impotence, depression, and so many other ills. You must connect yourself to the eternal source of power, Jesus Christ, who will set you up like a lighthouse on a hill. God's power is not temporal, seasonal, or faulty.

No need to change your batteries or look around for a jump start. It's not controlled by an external service provider, or the renewable energy of elements He created from the world's start.

Our lives are to be ministries guided by kingdom principles and activated faith. Everything we do as an individual, spouse, employee, entrepreneur, philanthropist, etc., should be guided by kingdom principles; not worldly norms, trends, and laws. When God says His people shall perish for a lack of knowledge, He is not speaking about the knowledge of the carnal world; and He is not speaking about knowledge that can be found on Google or Amazon. God is speaking about His eternal knowledge. You perish because you do not have any knowledge about who God is. You perish because you do not have any knowledge of who you were created to be. You perish because you do not have any knowledge about eternity. You perish because you are ignorant of God's language.

> You perish because you do not have any knowledge about who God is.

Instead of sowing into the ministry of God, many persons sow into the nail and hair salons. They convince themselves that all churches are set up to take their money, but they don't see how they've been set up to steal from God.

If you believe that life is simply a transaction, then what have you given to God for the priceless gift of life flowing through your veins? What have you done to deserve purpose or the talents you were gifted? – Instead of learning God's Word for yourself, you listen to false prophets or fall victim to every philosopher that casts doubt posed as logic. Is obedience to God too much to ask for when you who have children believe they owe their obedience to you? You try everything the world offers you for a better life, but you won't try Jesus because it's not gratifying enough for you.

> Is obedience to God too much to ask for when you who have children believe they owe their obedience to you?

Many people are walking around down trodden and struggling when they don't need to struggle because they have power. If you are, however, ignorant of the power you have inherited and do not know the language of God, how can you be powerful? Let God put his spirit on everything you read from the bible. Find God's word and stick it back in his face. God is not a liar and His word will never be made void.

Jesus Christ did not die on the Cross to gratify our flesh. When He took on the form of human flesh there was no gratification for Him. Jesus Christ came to die for our insidious and contaminating sins. His flesh was beaten, tortured, bruised, and killed for an undeserving humankind. He died so that we would have life eternally and abundantly. What God seeks to gratify us with, is His Holy Spirit who lives within us and makes us whole. Let us resolve to give unto God what He has deposited within our souls.

Every time, I face a dilemma, I think of what I believe in that situation and I would encourage you to do the same. If God is the maker of all things, you abide in Him, and His words abide in you; then you abide in all that He has created.

As I close in on my defence for belief in God, I would like to ask you three things. These three things serve to help you measure who, or what, you have believed in:

- **On a daily average, how much time do you spend thinking about God and learning about what He has said; by reading His Word and communicating with Him through prayer?**

In essence, I am asking, what investment of time have you made to sustain a relationship with God? Compared to how much time we spend on social media, with friends, family, and spouses, how much time do we actually give to knowing God and knowing what He wants for our lives?

- **What absorbs your heart and preoccupies your mind? Is it your relationship, job, career, family, education, science, technology, talents, giftings, religion, beauty, material riches, body, sex, sexuality, money, status quo, political affiliation, or God?**

Anything that takes precedence and sits on the throne of our hearts, over God, is an idol. Anything, but God, will bring temporary satisfaction and that is why we are always chasing after the next best thing. Ultimately, our idols will enslave us by making us dependent on the instant gratification it gives, but never satisfies. It's like eating our favourite cuisine: - we enjoy the "foodgasm" but by the time it's digested, we no longer feel satisfied. To get that satisfaction again, we will have to eat it again. That's what idols do to us. They incite us to keep coming back for more, to keep spending more, to keep searching for more. And yet in all our searching, we forget to search for God.

> *That's what idols do to us. They incite us to keep coming back for more, to keep spending more, to keep searching for more. And yet in all our searching, we forget to search for God.*

- **Is your current or intended purpose, or assignment, for your life connected to the eternal purposes of God or to the temporary present-day life of your flesh?**

Your gift is equipment for your assignment in life and a gift is not a gift until it is given. Being born is a gift in itself, but God has also gifted each and everyone of us with unique talents, abilities, capacities, opportunities, resources, purposes, and assignments. Have we tapped into God's eternal data centre? Have we plugged ourselves into God's eternal power source? Have we embraced ourselves as new creatures in Christ or have we just been playing with God?

> *Have we tapped into God's eternal data centre? Have we plugged ourselves into God's eternal power source?*

Let's normalize believing Jesus Christ. Let's stay woke in the Word of God. Let God trend in our humanistic pursuits. This is not an indictment. Rather, it is a clarion call for those who hear to begin doing as they've heard.

God understands that we are not perfect, but He is reminding us that we are accountable. We are answerable for our beliefs and so it is time we start asking ourselves:

"What do you believe?"

I've given you Scripture, Revelation, and my Experience.
Now it's your time to offer up your mindset to God.
New seeds will be sown, new roots will be developed,
and your tree will bring a harvest of good fruit
in spite of any storm.

ABOUT THE AUTHOR

Born and raised on the tropical Caribbean island of Tobago, Josanne Rojas is a blog writer, business professional and kingdom soldier. She posits herself to be a wife, mother to two boys, servant of God, and a friend. Her testimony is one of growing up in church, but not in God, and so when she received an ultimatum from God in 2018, she quickly transformed her life from one of rebellion to one of submission.

Mrs. Rojas is now focused on her God-given assignment to erode and destroy the stronghold of ignorance within the Body of Christ. In May 2021, Mrs. Rojas launched a blog called "Spiritual Literacy 101" to begin laying the blocks of the foundation of her Ministry.

Mrs. Rojas has always had a passion for the written word and grew up reading a great deal while writing poetry and songs. Even though her passion was ingrained in writing, she never saw being an author as a lucrative career choice coming from a small island state where writing was never presented as a wise or glorified career choice.

Mrs. Rojas once lived a life that was reckless and direction-less, but by God's grace, she has taken a leap in faith to trust God and pursue her dreams in a way that would glorify Him. She is an Ambassador for Christ and her mission is to empower others to live Christ centric lives.

Author's Contact:
Scarborough, Tobago, Trinidad & Tobago, W.I.
Tel: 1-868-729-5008
Email: josannerojas101@gmail.com

ACKNOWLEDGEMENTS

To my amorous and devoted husband –

In your wildest dreams, I know you never saw yourself being married to an author. Being the creative genius you are, I know you would like to take some credit for rubbing off some of that goodness on me. Thank you for putting up with my many late nights of reading and writing. It's just a part of the creative process.

I know you thought I was being super spiritual about my quarantine but after reading this book, I would really like to get your feedback on that my love. My time in quarantine was nothing short of comfortable, peaceful, and productive and I must thank you for ensuring that my time alone was first class in every way.

Thank you for loving me and going over and above to ensure that all of our family's needs are met. Your support and investment in my dreams is invaluable; and having you on this journey makes the ride even more worthwhile. ♥♥♥

To my dearest Lovellin–

You have always been incredibly encouraging and supportive of my writing. Actually, you've always been adamant that I get to know Jesus and you've always managed to see my heart. Thank you for not giving up on me. Your efforts in steering me on the narrow path were not in vain.

Thank you for proof-reading the rough versions of my book and for the time spent producing remarkable illustrations for my book. You are indeed irreplaceable.

To my cheerleader family (Mom/Patrick) –

Well I've finally done it! After all my years of writing poems of heartbreak and confusion, I believe I have produced something here that you can be proud of. This should compensate for the many years of waywardness you endured. Thank you for always being in my corner to cheer me on and for believing in me.

To Pastor Sonia Whitlock –

Pastor!!! Thank you for your stewardship, friendship, and counsel. Thank you for pushing me out of my comfort zone and for your unadulterated support. We are in this together!

To Dara Publishing –

Thank you for your confidence in this project. Your work and support as my publishing consultant has been brilliant. Our conversations have always been fruitful and I appreciate your frank transparency and commitment to my success as your client.

To Emeka Anslem –

To my Nigerian brother! Thank you for proofreading my book and for your tremendous feedback and support. You have been extremely generous with your time and counsel and I can always depend on you for some good emojis of laughter. Your books have been very inspiring and I'm hoping that your grace of speed and consistency in writing can fall upon me so that I can write that post you've challenged me to write one day as well.

To my close friends and inner circle –

I love all of you dearly and I am thankful that your support and loyalty has never wavered over the years. For some of you, this book may come as a surprise. For others, it may be another exploit you have to tarry with in the life of Josanne. Whichever way, I implore you to believe God and have your lives metamorphosized through His Word. That's the only treasure I can offer you that is long-lasting.

To my sons, Jaysean and Rome –

I dedicate this book to you both because there is nothing I want more than for you to know Jesus Christ for yourselves as you journey through this fallen world. I pray that one day you will grace the pages of this book with a yearning to know more about God and never live a life of ignorance.

Made in the USA
Columbia, SC
05 June 2023

17442564R00089